LEGENDS *of* FAITH

Famous HYMNWRITERS

Marilyn Boyer

First printing: November 2025

Master Books, P.O. Box 726, Green Forest, AR 72638

Master Books® is a division of the New Leaf Publishing Group, LLC.

ISBN: 978-1-68344-403-9
ISBN: 978-1-61458-990-7 (digital)
Library of Congress Control Number: pending

Printed in the United States of America

Visit our website for other great titles: www.masterbooks.com

For information regarding promotional opportunities, please contact the publicity department at pr@nlpg.com.

Master Books®
A Division of New Leaf Publishing Group
www.masterbooks.com

Table of Contents

Image Credits

Images created using Shutterstock AI and Firefly AI unless otherwise listed.

Hymns:

Pg 9: *The Hymnal Revised and Enlarged,* hymn 101

Pg 17: *Divine Songs,* Pages 18 and 19.

Pg 23: *Free Methodist Hymnal,* hymn 266

Pg 39: "Amazing Grace," Wikimedia

Pg 56: *Olney Hymns,* Wikimedia

Pg 61: *HYMNS: The Methodist Episcopal Church,* hymn 174

Pg 72: *The Church Hymn Book,* hymn 945

Pg 77: *Eternal Praise,* hymn 251

Pg 99: *It is Well with My Soul,* Wikimedia

Pg 115: *The Methodist Hymnal,* hymn 348

Pg 125: *Havergal's Psalmody*, title page

Pg 129: *Hymns of Consecration and Faith,* hymn 272

Pg 131: *Gospel Hymns No. 2,* hymn 7

Pg 147: *Gospel Hymn Selections For Female Voices No. 2,* hymn 1

Pg 157: *Gospel Songs, A choice collection of Hymns and Tunes,* hymn 59

Pg 161: library.timelesstruths.org

Introduction

What a treasure we have been given in the great old hymns! We are given instructions in Ephesians 5:19–20: "**Speaking to yourselves** in psalms and **hymns** and spiritual songs, singing and making melody in your heart to the Lord; **Giving thanks always** for **all things** unto God and the Father in the name of our Lord Jesus Christ (KJV)." The great hymns of the faith guide us to do just that.

These hymns are full of rich doctrine, blended with uplifting and often majestic tunes that help cement words of truth into our minds and hearts. In the very act of singing, we speak the truth to ourselves — something we must do daily. The world bombards our minds with untruths and selfish, unhealthy thoughts. Godly songs rich in the truth supplied in God's Word function to wash our minds and hearts and help us to think rightly. Notice how the tunes and words run through your head even when you are not trying to think of them. The singing of hymns leads us to meditate on truth.

Isaiah 55:6–13 tells us:

"Seek the Lord while he may be found;
call on him while he is near.

Let the wicked forsake their ways
and the unrighteous their thoughts.

Let them turn to the LORD, and he will have mercy on them,
and to our God, for he will freely pardon.

For my thoughts are not your thoughts,
neither are your ways my ways," declares the LORD.

“**As the heavens are higher than the earth**,
so are my ways higher than your ways
and my thoughts than your thoughts.

As the rain and the snow
come down from heaven,
and do not return to it
without watering the earth
and making it bud and flourish,
so that it yields seed for the sower and bread for the eater,
so is my word that goes out from my mouth:

It will not return to me empty,
but will accomplish what I desire
and achieve the purpose for which I sent it.

You will go out in joy
and be led forth in peace;
the mountains and hills
will **burst into song** before you,
and all the trees of the field
will clap their hands.

Instead of the thornbush will grow the juniper,
and instead of briers, the myrtle will grow.

This will be for the LORD’s renown,
for an everlasting sign,
that will endure forever (NIV).”

Singing truth helps us exchange our natural thoughts for God’s thoughts that guide us every day. Many of our hymns cause us to worship the one, true, and holy God. In some hymns, we express praise and thankfulness to God. In others, we meditate on truths found in Scripture. As we lift our voices in praise, we receive encouragement from them. In the very act of singing, we teach, admonish, comfort, counsel, and guide one another, and thus fulfill the command of Ephesians 5. It is a commendable practice to make singing a hymn part of our daily routine. It makes good sense when you are feeling down to sing a great old hymn of the faith. Needless to say, it makes good sense to sing when you are feeling joyous. God takes pleasure in His people offering Him praise!

It is amazing to see how so many of the authors of the hymns wrote while going through times of great suffering. God delights in using our trials to bless us and others. He takes what we consider to be bad and turns it into good for His glory. Knowing their stories supplies an added depth to the richness of the words and tunes.

Note that some Hymnwriters wrote words only. Some supplied music only, and some composed both, but all are considered to be Hymnwriters. It's amazing to see how so many of their paths crossed in life and how they encouraged and supported one another. Isn't heaven going to be incredible! We will see how others influenced our lives in ways we never knew. We will learn how our lives were used to encourage others. Best of all, we will learn how God fit all the puzzle pieces together to create a masterpiece of grace for eternity. Hope you enjoy the stories!

1

Isaac Watts

The Father of English Hymnwriting

.D. 1400 1450 1500 1550 1600 1650 1674–1748 1800 1850

"Love so amazing, so divine, Demands my soul, my life, my all."

Hymn: "When I Survey the Wondrous Cross"

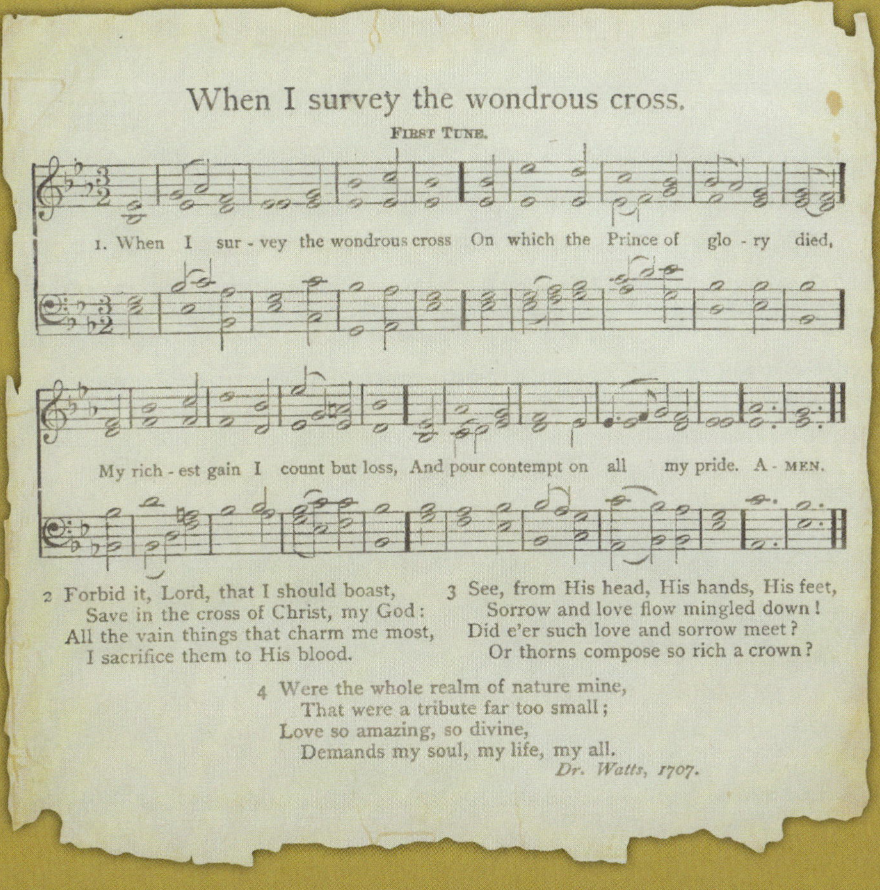

When I survey the wondrous cross.

FIRST TUNE.

1. When I sur - vey the wondrous cross On which the Prince of glo - ry died,

My rich - est gain I count but loss, And pour contempt on all my pride. A - MEN.

2 Forbid it, Lord, that I should boast,
Save in the cross of Christ, my God:
All the vain things that charm me most,
I sacrifice them to His blood.

3 See, from His head, His hands, His feet,
Sorrow and love flow mingled down!
Did e'er such love and sorrow meet?
Or thorns compose so rich a crown?

4 Were the whole realm of nature mine,
That were a tribute far too small;
Love so amazing, so divine,
Demands my soul, my life, my all.

Dr. Watts, 1707.

Who Was Isaac Watts?

Isaac Watts was an English Congregational pastor. He grew up with a special gift from God to produce poetry. From the time he was a boy, he thought in rhyme and **meter**. In his day, people sang only the Psalms in church. Isaac felt the hymns sung were rather tunelessly and mentioned this to his father. "His father smiled and suggested that he provide something better."[1] At 18, he aimed to do this. His first hymn was "Behold the Glories of the Lamb." His aim in producing Christian hymns was to enable God's people to sing His Word in the form of beautiful poetry. He composed over 700 hymns in his lifetime. Among his most beloved hymns are: "When I Survey the Wondrous Cross" and "O God, Our Help in Ages Past."

The Early Years

Isaac Watts was born on July 17, 1674, in Southampton, England. His father Isaac Watts Sr. was a **Nonconformist** deacon at the Above Bar Congregational Chapel, pastored by Reverend Nathaniel Robinson. When Isaac was born, his father was in prison for failing to conform to the **Anglican Church**. The king and Parliament were determined to punish those who refused to attend Anglican services. First, they established fines. Next, they often seized property or put offenders in prison. Some were even put to death by hanging. When married only a year, his father served his first prison term. It would not be his last. During this time, his mother gave birth to Isaac. She

meter: a basic repeated pattern of rhythm or music

Nonconformist: one who did not conform to certain practices of the established church and was therefore restricted from many areas of public life

Anglican Church: the established church in England

would sit on a stone block in front of the prison and nurse young Isaac while she talked with his father through the prison bars. Sarah was the daughter of Alderman Taunton, whose **Huguenot** ancestors had escaped to England in 1572 seeking religious freedom. She was no stranger to persecution.

> **Huguenot:** French protestant
>
> **clothier:** a maker of woolen cloth

Early Instruction

When he was not behind bars, Isaac's father was a **clothier**. He also ran a boarding school in their home. His school developed a reputation for academic excellence. Students would come from America and the West Indies to receive an education from Isaac Watts Sr.

Young Isaac was taught at home. His father began to teach him Latin when he was only four years old. He later mastered Greek, distortions: altering something true

Hebrew, and French. His father wanted to protect his children from **distortions** of the Gospel, which had crept into the Anglican church practices. He admonished them, "You must receive no doctrine, but such is rightly built upon the Holy Scriptures. My children, pray to God to give you the knowledge of the truth and to keep you from error, for it is a very dangerous time you are to live in."[2]

Love of Poetry

Love of poetry had been a part of the Watts family for generations. One evening as his father was leading in family worship, young Isaac, eyeing a mouse, began laughing. When asked why, he replied with a rhyme, "There was a mouse for want of stairs; Ran up a rope to say his prayers."[3] His parents were amazed at his early ability to produce rhymes in his head. His father got exasperated with his constant rhyming at one point and forbade him to continue. Isaac forgot and when faced with receiving a switching, he pled,
"O father, do some mercy take; And I will no more verses make."[4]

In the future, the talent that often annoyed Isaac's parents would continue to flourish and be used by God to bless millions of Christians through his hymns. When he was only seven years old, he wrote a poem that was an **acrostic** of his name. It reflected an incredible depth of understanding of doctrine. Young Isaac had a sincere love for books. Whenever he had any money to spend, he begged his mother to buy another book. Encouraged by his father, he learned to cherish the Word of God above all books.

acrostic: a poem in which the first letters in each line form a word

Teen Years

Isaac attended the Free School in Southampton as a teen. He sat under the Reverend John Pinhorne, who trained his students to know God through a personal relationship with Jesus Christ. One Sunday in 1690, on the way home from church, Isaac expressed his disapproval of the "ugly" way the hymns were sung in church. "The singing of God's praise is the part of worship highest heaven, but its performance among us is the worst on earth."[5] His father gently rebuked him, saying, "If you do not like the hymns, young man, then give us something better."[6] That very afternoon, Isaac wrote a hymn of eight stanzas based on Revelation 5:6-12. When he came downstairs, he presented it to his father. Very impressed, Mr. Watts took it to the Independent Chapel that evening. The hymn was enthusiastically received. Isaac was encouraged to write more. He wrote a new song for each Sunday for the next two years.

Preparing for the Ministry

Isaac attended Newington Academy in London when he was 16 years old. Reverend Thomas Rowe was the director of the academy and pastor of the Nonconformist church Isaac attended. Isaac learned to carefully study the Bible and prepare sermons as well as learning math, history, sciences, geography, rhetoric, ethics, and anatomy. Isaac loved his teacher and wrote a poem as a tribute to him. Isaac developed a lot of lifetime friendships while there. He and his friends sat under many great preachers while in London. He also spent much time studying the Word of God and writing.

He graduated at 20 years old and returned home for two and a half years. In 1696, he took the position of tutor in the home of a wealthy nonconformist. Here, he learned the skill of communicating truth to children. He loved teaching children. When speaking to teachers, he said, "Youth is the time for acquiring knowledge and as you have the important charge laid upon you of instructing some of the rising generation, let me beg that you will leave nothing undone to make your pupils love the beauties of religion. Teach them that religion has nothing in it of a gloomy nature, for how can that be gloomy which leads to everlasting pleasures?"[7]

Isaac also continued to write hymns. On his 24th birthday, he was called to preach at Mark Lane Chapel, one of the most influential pulpits at the time. The congregation had been dwindling under poor leadership, but quickly responded to Watts' passionate preaching style. It was not long before they called him to preach every week. Watts began writing a hymn weekly to illustrate the message he was preaching. He never entered the pulpit without bathing his sermon in much prayer. He described prayer as "a conversation with God above while we are here below."[8] He loved visiting his congregation in their homes and was especially tender to children and the poor. In 1703, due to his poor health, the congregation hired an assistant, Samuel Price, who helped him for the remainder of his ministry. The congregation grew quickly from 75 people to more than 500. Eventually, they had to move to a larger building on Bury Street.

palatial: splendid

lord mayor: a title of a mayor of a major city with special recognition by the king

Watts Becomes Ill

In 1712, Isaac became so sick with a fever, various stomach ailments, and headaches that he could no longer preach. He had tried many cures. He visited his home in Southampton and the countryside in Bath and Turnbridge, hoping the fresh air would help. He even purchased a horse, and in eight months rode more than 800 miles. He would have brief periods of relief, but the illness always returned. He was invited to recover in Sir Thomas Abney's **palatial** estate. Abney was the one-time **lord mayor** of London, and he appointed Watts to be his personal chaplain and tutor for his children. The one week of rest and recovery turned into 36 years! He continued to ride into the city to preach when able, but always returned to Abney Park to rest and to continue writing. He would often climb the hill and look out over the vast estate and do his writing there. They later named the hill Watts Mount.

Productive Servant

Although burdened by illness, Watts was very productive with his time. He was determined to use his gift of writing to show others the glories of his Savior and the forgiveness of sin found in Christ alone. He wrote more than 50 books during those years. More importantly, he composed 750 hymns! His best-known work was *Hymns and Spiritual Songs*, which was comprised of three books. It was first published in 1707, although expanded upon in later years. It was the first real hymnbook in the English language. "Before this only Psalms were sung in church, but he saw no reason why Christian praise should be confined to the actual language of the Bible. Watts sought to make it possible for God's people to sing His Word in the form of good poetry."[9] Watts' hymns have been called rhymed sermons. Those who sing his hymns are "dazzled with the splendor of Christ and the Gospel."[10]

Isaac Watts — Hymnwriter

The hymns of Isaac Watts set a new pattern for future Hymnwriters. He interpreted the Old Testament using the knowledge we learn in the New Testament. He described his method here: “Where the Psalmist describes religion by the fear of God, I have often joined faith and love to it. Where he speaks of pardon of sin through the mercies of God, I have added the merits of a Saviour. Where he talks of sacrificing goats and bullocks, I rather mention the sacrifice of Christ, the Lamb of God. When he attends the ark with shouting into Zion, I sing of the ascension of my Saviour into heaven, or His presence in His church on earth. Where he promises abundance of wealth, honor, and long life, I have changed some of these typical blessings for grace, glory, and life eternal, which are brought to light in the Gospel, and promised in the New Testament.”[11]

Watts became famous for *Divine Songs Attempted in Easy Language for the Use of Children*, published in 1719. His purpose as told in the preface was to teach children to delight in learning the truths of Scripture. He determined to teach students a song each week to help them retain precious truths of the Word. It is an amazing collection of instructive songs teaching children the blessings of diligence, obedience to parents, carefully guarding the words they speak, exhortations to be honest, how to give their best to

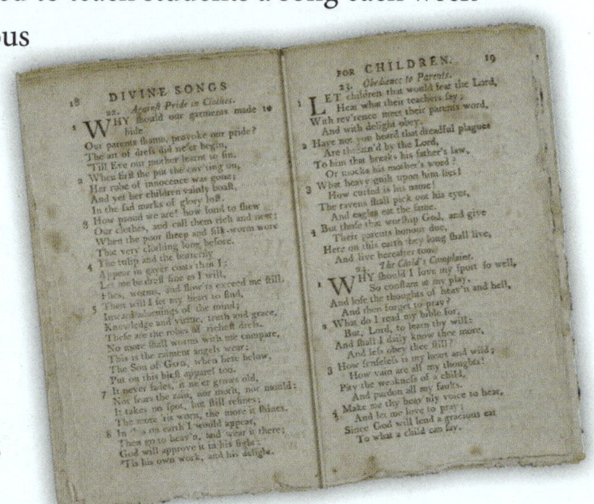

God while still young, and many foundational truths about God. For example, here is part of one song:

> "O may that Spirit teach
> And make my heart receive
> Those truths which all Thy servants preach,
> And all thy saints believe.
> Then shall I praise the Lord
> In a more cheerful strain,
> That I was taught to read His Word,
> And have not learnt in vain."[12]

His songbook was used by God to shape more than two generations of children in both America and England. As he stated, "What is learned in verse is longer retained in memory, and sooner recollected and may prove to be an effectual means to keep off some temptation or to incline to some duty."[13]

Among the hymns Watts wrote that have remained favorites throughout the years are: "Alas and Did My Savior Bleed," "Am I a Soldier of the Cross," "Come We That Love the Lord," "How Sweet and Awful Is the Place," "I Sing the Mighty Power of God," "Joy to the World, the Lord Is Come," "O God Our Help in Ages Past," and "When I Survey the Wondrous Cross."

Watts' Influence in America

> **wadding:** pieces of cloth or paper used between the powder and the bullet to prevent it from dropping into the powder charge, holding it in place in the barrel

During the Great Awakening, Watts' hymns were widely sung and used by God to fuel revival in the colonies. George Whitefield used Watts' hymns while preaching outdoors from Georgia through New England. Jonathan Edwards studied Watts' sermons and used his hymns regularly. Preacher Samuel Davies had copies of his hymns printed and distributed to African slaves in the American colonies. He used them to teach slaves in his congregation how to read. Davies told how "his kitchen would be full late into the night with slaves who had gathered to sing Watts."[14]

On June 23, 1780, General Nathaniel Greene and his 2,000-man regiment were in a fierce battle with 6,000 British at the Battle of Springfield in New Jersey. Suddenly, the New Jersey patriots ran out of **wadding** for their muskets. A musket is useless without wadding. Reverend James Caldwell, a pastor whose wife had been recklessly

killed by the British just a few weeks before, ran to his church. He returned with his arms loaded with the well-known Isaac Watts hymnals. He began tearing out the pages of the beloved hymnals, shouting to the soldiers, "Give 'em Watts! Put Watts into 'em, boys!"[15] The men used the pages of the hymnals as wadding and won a victory that day, even though they were severely outnumbered.

Prepared for Death

Watts struggled with poor health so often that he faced the possibility of death throughout his life. He felt a compulsion to prepare others to be ready to face death, as much of the population died at an early age from disease. Through his hymns, he taught hope and courage when faced with death. He pointed others to the dear Christ who conquered death for those for whom He died. He was always mindful of the poor.

Watts gained very little profit from the books he wrote. Samuel Johnson in *Lives of the Poets* tells us that Watts gave to the poor "the third part of his annual revenues, though the whole was not a hundred pounds a year."[16]

On his deathbed, Watts told his personal secretary, "The most learned and knowing Christians, when they come to die, have only the same plain promises of the Gospel for their support, as the common and unlearned; and so I find it. They are the plain promises of the Gospel which are my support."[17]

Isaac Watts died peacefully on November 25, 1748, in the Abney Park home. He was 74. He was buried in the nonconformist cemetery of Bunhill Fields in London. His hymns are still greatly loved, and Isaac Watts is honored even today. If you were to visit Southampton Civic Centre in Watts' Park today, you would hear the clock chime the tune of the opening line of "O God, Our Help in Ages Past" three times a day, at 8 a.m., noon, and 4 p.m.

Isaac Watts revolutionized church music. It may best be told by his brother Enoch, who had tried to convince the reluctant Isaac to publish his hymns early on. "There is a great need of a pen, vigorous and lively as yours, to quicken and revive the dying devotion of the age."[18] Christians from every age now reap the benefit of such a gifted Hymnwriter. May we all marvel at Christ and give our devotion to Him as we sing with added understanding the majestic song for which he is so famous.

2

Charles Wesley

Powerful & Prolific Hymnwriter

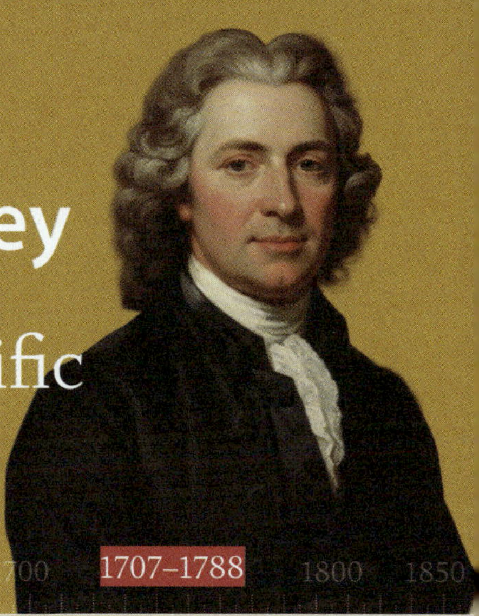

D. 1450 1500 1550 1600 1650 1700 1707–1788 1800 1850

"Amazing love! How can it be? That thou, my God, shouldst die for me?"

Hymn: "And Can It Be"

266 L. M. 61.

AND can it be that I should gain
An interest in the Savior's blood?
Died he for me, who caused his pain?
For me, who him to death pursued?
Amazing love! how can it be
That thou, my Lord, shouldst die for me?

2 'Tis mystery all! the Immortal dies!
Who can explore his strange design?
In vain the first-born seraph tries
To sound the depths of love divine;
'Tis mercy all! let earth adore:
Let angel minds inquire no more.

3 He left his Father's throne above,
So free, so infinite his grace!
Emptied himself of all but love,
And bled for Adam's helpless race;
'Tis mercy all, immense and free,
For, O my God, it found out me!

4 Long my imprisoned spirit lay,
Fast bound in sin and nature's night;
Thine eye diffused a quickening ray;
I woke; the dungeon flamed with light:
My chains fell off, my heart was free,
I rose, went forth, and followed thee.

5 No condemnation now I dread,
Jesus, with all in him, is mine;
Alive in him, my living Head,
And clothed in righteousness divine,
Bold I approach the eternal throne,
And claim the crown, through Christ, my own.

Charles Wesley.

163

Who Was Charles Wesley?

Charles Wesley was an English preacher who, along with his brother John, was credited for having begun the Methodist movement. Even more importantly, he wrote over 8,000 Christian hymns in his lifetime, an average of three hymns per week over 50 years. His hymns are rich in theology and inspire those who sing them to praise the one true God and His Son, Jesus Christ. He endured much opposition to his preaching but persevered, leading thousands to a saving knowledge of Jesus Christ.

prematurely: before his due date

Early Years — The Christmas Baby

Charles was the 18th of the 19 children of Samuel and Susanna Wesley. He was born on Christmas Day, 1707, a month **prematurely**. The infant was weak and small, and it was feared that he would not survive infancy. In mid-January, about the time he should have been born, he opened his eyes and started to cry, and from that time on began to thrive. His brother John was four years old when Charles

was born. The two remained close throughout their lives. When Charles was 14 months old, the family's house caught fire. The servant girl grabbed baby Charles, and thankfully, the entire family escaped without harm. Neighbors offered space in their homes for the Wesleys until their house could be rebuilt; nevertheless, this event put the family in a tight financial situation.

impeccable: flawless

Fellow: highly respected teacher

The children were taught at home in their early years by their mother. They all learned to read at a young age and were brought up with godly disciplines of Bible reading and daily prayer. They were taught to have **impeccable** manners and to treat each other with kindness.

School Days

In 1716, Charles, only eight years old, was sent to Westminster School in London. He was able to stay with his oldest brother Samuel and his family. Samuel was almost like Charles' second father. Charles was a good student, studying Greek and Latin. At 18, he was awarded a King's Scholarship to attend Christ Church in Oxford. His brother John had just become a **Fellow** of Lincoln College at Oxford. Charles would often burst into John's room to share a new poem he had written.

John encouraged Charles to be diligent in his pursuit of pleasing God, although neither of the brothers had a saving faith at this time. They both sought to please God by diligence, study, and works of righteousness. Charles befriended a couple of like-minded students. They met each week to read the Bible and pray together. John joined them, became their leader, and formed "The Holy Club."

The Holy Club

The four friends began visiting and preaching to prisoners in the Castle Prison, many of whom were sentenced to be put to death. The Holy Club grew over the next couple of years. Soon, nine men were attending the meetings, including George Whitefield. They ministered to the poor in the city and taught neglected children to read and write. They cared for sick and needy folks. They distributed Bibles and prayer books when they had enough money to purchase them.

The Holy Club members sought to order their lives. They arose early each day, fasted on Wednesdays and Fridays, and prayed together each day at 9 a.m., noon, and 3 p.m., as well as having individual prayer times. They determined to show kindness to everyone and pray for those with various needs. The other students ridiculed them and called them Methodists because they desired to practice methodical lifestyles. At this time in their lives, they were attempting to please God and earn salvation rather than trusting Christ's finished work on the Cross.

In April 1735, Charles' and John's father Samuel was dying. As Charles leaned forward to pray for his father, Samuel put his hand on Charles' head and proclaimed, "The Christian faith will surely revive in this kingdom. You shall see it, but I shall not."[19] Little did Samuel realize that God would use his two sons to spark a spiritual revival in England and Ireland.

Missionaries in America

First, though, both John and Charles were invited by Colonel James Oglethorpe to join him in America. Oglethorpe was a former soldier and member of Parliament. He had a burden for poor debtors who were imprisoned for not paying their debts. He obtained their release by coming up with a solution: He established a colony in America named Georgia after the King of England, George II. Newly released prisoners who had some kind of skills were invited to get a fresh start in the New World.

The Society for the Propagation of the Gospel, the official missionary society of the Church of England, offered John Wesley a chaplaincy in Savannah, Georgia. It included a decent salary. John begged his brother Charles to accompany him. He encouraged Charles to seek **ordination** from the Church of England before they left. They then found two other men to join them in their mission. Charles was assigned the role of Secretary for Indian Affairs as well as personal secretary to Colonel Oglethorpe.

ordination: officially setting apart for ministry

Off for America

On October 14, 1735, the group departed for America. John kept a journal of how the men spent their time during the journey. As was their custom, they were very methodical and disciplined. Bible study, prayer, and preaching to the 80 people on board made up a typical day. They experienced two fearful storms that caused both Charles and John to wonder if they really did know Jesus as the Savior and Lord of their lives. There was a group of **Moravian believers** on board who took the storm in stride, trusting their lives to God.

Moravian believers: Moravian Church beliefs are solidly grounded in the Bible, under the teachings of Czech reformer John Huss

reproached: disgraced, shame

John and Charles felt **reproached** by the Moravians' faith. They questioned if they genuinely trusted God as an ever-present help in trouble. One of the Moravian pastors asked John, "Does the Spirit of God bear witness with your spirit that you are a child of God?"[20]

Neither John nor Charles had an answer. Although they thought they were going to America to share the Gospel with the Indians and the poor, God had plans to bring them closer to a saving knowledge of Himself. They were still depending on their good works to save them.

Ministry in America

Oglethorpe sent Charles to St. Simon's Island, 100 miles south of Savannah, while John remained in the capital city. Charles set to work ministering to the local inhabitants. Oglethorpe expected Charles to spend most of his time as the colonel's personal assistant. This job would have suited John much better than Charles, however, because John, not Charles, had a gift for organization and administration.

Charles felt compelled to teach his parishioners to live holy, disciplined lives as he had always attempted to do. However, the settlers did not respond well to a works-based religion. Charles' sermons were focused on sin and God's punishment — the settlers did not like that either. Charles had never dreamed he would have such difficult struggles. He became very ill, and John, hearing about it, came quickly to his aid. Shortly after Charles recovered, Oglethorpe decided to send him back to England to assure the Board of Trustees that the new colony was prospering. Charles was thrilled to leave. On July 26, 1736, he boarded a ship for England. In November 1737, John followed Charles back to England.

Both Charles and John had repeatedly written to George Whitefield, encouraging him to consider coming to America. While they were headed back to England, George was on his way to America. Charles and John were responsible for George Whitefield going to America; George Whitefield was the **impetus** behind **The Great Awakening** in America. Charles and John would soon be delivered from a religion of works.

impetus: driving force

Great Awakening: a series of religious revivals

providentially: happening from divine intervention

pleurisy: an illness of the lungs causing pain in breathing

The Brothers Come to Salvation

In February 1738, Peter Boehler, a Moravian missionary headed for Georgia, **providentially** came to stay with the Wesley brothers for three months. He knew Latin but very little English. He asked Charles to tutor him in preparation for leaving for America. During this time, Boehler lost no time in teaching Charles and John about salvation by faith alone. Seeds were being sown.

Just one week after Boehler left for the colonies, Charles was compelled to move to another location in town, the home of Mr. Bray. At first, Charles thought Mr. Bray was just an ignorant mechanic, but soon saw he had misjudged him. Charles became terribly ill with **pleurisy**. During the next nine days, Charles became increasingly sick. Mr. Bray knew Jesus Christ personally and prayed with Charles, reading to him from the Bible. Also, at this time, another friend loaned Charles a copy of Martin Luther's book, *Commentary on Galatians*. Luther wrote about justification by faith. Because of both influences, on May 21, 1738, Charles opened his Bible to Psalm 40:3: "He put a new song in my mouth, a song of praise to our God. Many will see and fear and put their trust in the Lord." At last, all the seeds that had been planted came to fruition. That night, Charles wrote in his journal, "I now found myself at peace with God, and rejoiced in hope of loving Christ … I saw that by faith I stood."[21]

Two days later, Charles began writing a song to celebrate his conversion. Mr. Bray encouraged him to finish it. God had been working in John's heart as well. John Wesley burst into Charles' room three days afterward and announced, "I believe, I believe!"[22] Hugging his brother, Charles exclaimed, "We must sing praise to God! Look here, brother, I have written a new song."[23] John excitedly read the words. "Yes, yes, my chains fell off, my heart was free! Such wonderful words!"[24] He exclaimed, "Oh my dearest brother Charles. Splendid. Lead us in this new song."[25] Together they sang for the first time this hymn that has blessed millions since:

"And Can It Be"
And can it be,
that I should gain an interest in the Savior's blood?
Died he for me, who caused his pain?
For me who him to death pursued?
Amazing love!
How can it be that thou, my God, shouldst die for me?
Amazing love!
How can it be that thou, my God, shouldst die for me?
He left his Father's throne above,
so free, so infinite his grace!
Emptied himself of all but love,
and bled for Adam's helpless race!
'Tis mercy all, immense and free,
for O, my God, it found out me.
Amazing love! How can it be?

That thou, my God, shouldst die for me?
Long my imprisoned spirit lay fast
bound in sin and nature's night.
Thine eye diffused a quickening ray;
I woke—the dungeon flamed with light!
My chains fell off, my heart was free,
I rose, went forth, and followed thee.
Amazing love! How can it be that thou,
my God, shouldst die for me?
No condemnation now I dread;
Jesus and all in him is mine!
Alive in him, my living Head,
and clothed in righteousness divine,
Bold, I approach the eternal throne and claim the crown
through Christ my own.
Amazing love!
How can it be that thou, my God, shouldst die for me?

The Gospel Is Proclaimed

foundry: a factory that produces metal castings by melting, pouring, and solidifying metals into molds

George Whitefield returned to England to raise money for orphanages in America. Church of England pulpits opposed him and were closed to their new Methodist style of preaching. So, Whitefield, John, and Charles began preaching in open-air meetings, which were heavily attended.

They obtained an old, abandoned **foundry**, that had been previously used to make cannons. John obtained a lease for the building, and the Methodists began renovating it.

The building could seat 1,500 people. They used one of the rooms to hold Bible classes. One end of the room was turned into a classroom, and the other end was used for a bookroom. Here, they trained Methodist **itinerate** preachers. Charles and John used the building as their headquarters. They, along with the preachers they trained, began spreading out and evangelizing all over England.

itinerate: one who travels from place to place

Charles had the unique gift of drawing people in through his preaching and hymn writing. He often composed new hymns after significant events in his life. Once, Peter Boehler remarked to Charles, "If I had one thousand tongues, I'd praise Christ with them all."[26] These words impressed Charles so much that a year later, he sat down and wrote that well-loved hymn,

"O For a Thousand Tongues to Sing"
O for a thousand tongues to sing
My great Redeemer's praise
The glories of my God and King,
The triumphs of His grace.

Opposition

Charles did not preach without opposition. On occasion, rioters threw stones at him, sometimes hitting him in the face. It did not stop him from preaching. Charles said that the Lord was his strength. At times, he was held up by highwaymen, and he was often hampered by the weather. For more than 15 years, he rode "all over Bristol and the west country, down into Devon and Cornwall, across to Cardiff and Wales, up in Staffordshire, and across to Durham. He rode the circuit and preached in Newcastle, Epworth, and Wiltshire."[27]

At the beginning of his ministry in Ireland, violent mobs opposed him, but after two months, people's hearts softened to his message. The mayor of Dublin announced that he would imprison anyone who verbally abused the Methodists. In his journal, Charles wrote, '

"God had begun a great work here. The people of Tyril's-pass were wicked to a proverb; swearers, drunkards, Sabbath-breakers, thieves, etc. from time immemorial. But now the scene is entirely changed. Not an oath is heard, or a drunkard seen among them. They are turned from darkness into light. Near one hundred are joined in Society and following hard after the pardoning of God."[28]

Charles Marries

While visiting a clergyman's house in Garth, Charles met Miss Sally Gwynne. Charles felt immediately drawn to Sally, but he was headed to minister in Ireland for six months. When he returned, he intended to stop at Garth. He did, but due to riding in a drenching rainstorm, he arrived sick. The Gwynne family took him in and kindly nursed him back to health. Here, his relationship with Sally grew. Charles and Sally were married on April 8, 1749. His brother John conducted the service. Charles' ministry, now that he was married, centered mostly around Bristol and London. Over the years, he and Sally had eight children, although only three survived. All three children shared their father's love for music.

Composing Hymns

Charles wrote and published thousands of hymns and poems. Among the most loved and well-known hymns he wrote are: "Christ the Lord is Risen Today," "And Can It Be," "Come, Thou Long Expected Jesus," "Hark! The Herald Angels Sing," "Jesus, Lover of my Soul," "Love Divine, All Loves Excelling," "O For a Thousand Tongues to Sing," and "Rejoice the Lord is King!" Due to poor health, Charles discontinued his traveling ministry in 1756,

but he never stopped composing hymns. He wrote 56 volumes of hymns in the 53 years between his ordination and his death. His hymns have blessed countless generations.

Henry Ward Beecher, who lived a century later, once said about his favorite: "Jesus, Lover of My Soul," "I would rather have written that hymn of Wesley's … than to have the fame of all the kings that ever sat on earth."[29]

Charles Wesley is Promoted to Heaven

In January 1788, Charles grew weak and was confined to bed. His devoted, loving wife Sally often sat by his bed reading the Bible to him. One day in late March, she read from her Bible: "So we do not lose heart. Though our outer self is wasting away, our inner self is being renewed day by day. For this light momentary affliction is preparing us for an eternal weight of glory beyond all comparison, as we look not to the things that are seen but to the things that are unseen. For the things that are seen are transient, but the things that are unseen are eternal …" (2 Corinthians 4:16-18, ESV). Charles said, "Amen." Then he asked her to write something for him, as he was too weak to lift his pen. He dictated to Sally his last poem.

"In age and feebleness extreme
Who shall a sinful worm redeem?
Jesus, my only hope Thou art,
Strength of my failing flesh and heart;
Oh, could I catch a smile from Thee,
And drop into eternity!"[30]

Charles lapsed into unconsciousness. On March 29, 1788, surrounded by his loving family, Charles Wesley entered eternity to see the face of his beloved Redeemer. The last verse of "Love Divine, All Loves Excelling" became a reality for Charles:

"Finish then Thy new creation, pure and spotless let us be,
Let us see Thy great salvation perfectly restored in Thee
Changed from glory into glory,
till in heaven we take our place
Till we cast our crowns before Thee,
lost in wonder, love and praise."

John Newton

From Slaver to Preacher

.D. 1450 1500 1550 1600 1650 1700 **1725–1807** 1850 1900

"Amazing grace, how sweet the sound, That saved a wretch like me..."

Hymn: "Faith's Review and Expectation"; best known as "Amazing Grace"

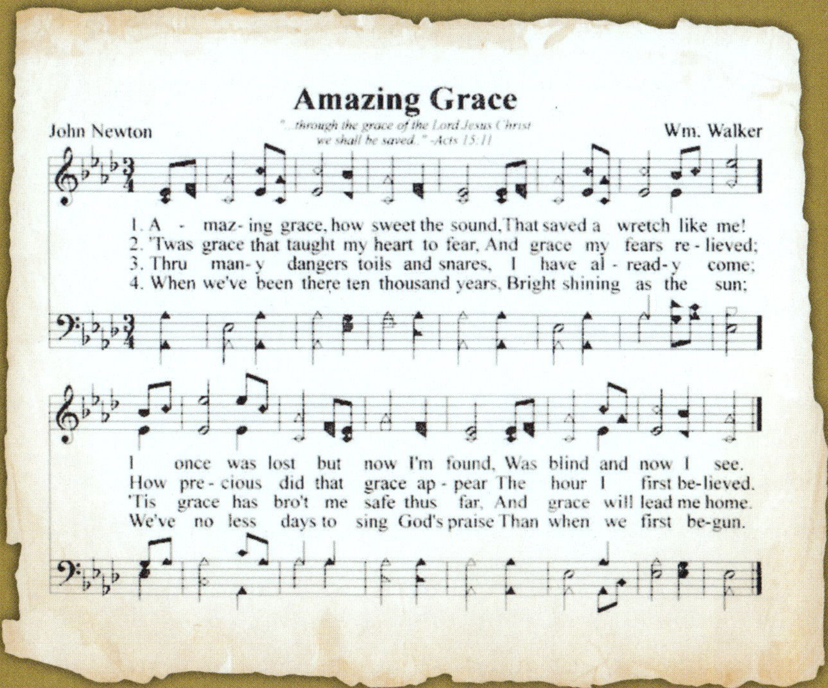

Who Was John Newton?

John Newton was an English slave trader who became an Anglican minister. Later, he joined forces with **William Wilberforce** to influence Parliament to abolish slavery in England. He wrote over 280 hymns and is best known for his hymn "Amazing Grace," which some consider the world's most famous hymn. This song was inspired by his transformation from a **wretched** seaman to a man of deep faith. Other beloved hymns include "Glorious Things of Thee Are Spoken," "I Asked the Lord," and "How Sweet the Name of Jesus Sounds."

William Wilberforce: a British politician who led the fight to abolish slavery and the slave trade in British possessions

wretched: extremely bad or distressed

Dissenting: Protestants who separated from the Church of England

Westminster Shorter Catechism: a concise summary of Christian doctrine formulated in the 17th century, primarily aimed at instructing children

Early Life

John was born on July 24, 1725. His father was a sea captain and spent much time away from home. His mother Elizabeth was a devout Christian who faithfully took John to a **Dissenting** church. He later recalled having liked singing a new hymn by Isaac Watts: "When I Survey the Wondrous Cross." His mother consistently taught him from the Bible. She had him memorize the **Westminster Shorter Catechism**. She loved her son dearly and taught him to read by the time he was three years old. She instructed him in Latin and had him memorize Isaac Watts' *Divine Songs for Children*. She hoped that one day, he would become a preacher. She wanted him to attend Saint Andrew's University in Scotland to train for the ministry when he grew up.

John's mother had been sick ever since he could remember. She would often teach him as she lay in bed suffering from fits of coughing. He heard her tell her pastor that she had consumption, a disease of the lungs, now known as tuberculosis. They lived in Wapping, located by the Thames River in London. Many factories nearby filled the air with **acrid** smoke. Combined with the ever-present fog of the city, the sunlight hardly ever shone through.

acrid: a strong, unpleasant, irritating smell

John Loses His Mother

One day, when John was six years old, his mother's distant cousin, Elizabeth Catlett, came to visit. She decided that if John's mother had any hope of recovery, she must have fresh sea air. John watched as she bundled up his beloved mother — his dearest friend — and helped her into the carriage. Cousin Elizabeth was a kind woman. She fully intended to nurse John's mother back to health. At first, John expected to accompany his mother, but she told him tearfully that he must stay and wait for his father to return from

the sea. As the carriage headed down the road for Chatham, Kent, where the Catletts lived, John felt totally alone. He had never really known his stern father, and he could not imagine life apart from his mother. He continued to do his chores and attend church. He learned large portions of the Westminster catechism, knowing this would please his mother. On July 13, 1732, John, now seven, received the terrible news that his mother died.

Life Changes for John

When John's father finally did return home, he heard the sad news about his wife. He left again but just a few weeks later, came back with a new wife. His new wife did not want to live in the city, so they moved 15 miles east to the countryside in Essex. Here, they lived on the farm that belonged to his wife's father. John was given farm chores, and his father headed off again to sea. His new stepmother could not read and had no regard for schooling or religion. She had no interest in John either. When John turned eight, his father enrolled him in a boarding school in Stratford, 20 miles away. John did well in school. He still hoped to be able to attend Saint Andrew's University, but his father only paid for two years of schooling. After that, he made John join him on a ship as a cabin boy.

John Becomes a Cabin Boy

John soon learned that a cabin boy was given very **menial** tasks. John was determined to continue to pray and read his Bible daily as his mother taught him. He even decided to recite his favorite Isaac Watts hymns in bed

menial: lowly

each night. He soon found, though, that an immense struggle was unfolding within him. On the one hand, he wanted to follow the good disciplines he had learned, but on the other, the rough lives of the sailors had an attraction for him.

John's first voyage lasted nine months. Upon returning home, he found that his father's new wife had given birth to a baby while they were gone. His father and his wife **doted on** the new son, and John felt terribly unloved.

doted on: gave lots of attention

During these years, a couple of incidents happened that impressed John with the truth that God was watching over him. On one occasion, he was thrown from his step-grandfather's horse. He landed on the ground just inches away from a stiff hawthorn stick that came close to poking out his eye. The second experience occurred when he was unexpectedly detained at home and prevented from joining friends on a particular outing. Because of that, he was saved from a drowning accident. These events sobered John, and he committed again to faithfully read his Bible.

Back to the Sea

John's father returned and once more took John to sea, this time as a seaman. John was now 14 years old. He was greatly influenced by the coarse lives of his fellow sailors, and the battle again raged within him. In November 1742, Captain Newton arranged with his friend, Joseph Manesty, a ship's captain from Liverpool, for John to take a position as slave **overseer** on a Jamaican plantation. This would allow John to become a plantation owner before he was 30 years old. John eagerly accepted. He thought that in 20 years, he could most likely retire a wealthy man. He packed his bags and awaited the ship taking him to Jamaica.

In the meantime, while John was waiting, his father sent him on an errand delivering some papers 30 miles away. One day before leaving on this errand, John received a letter from his cousin Elizabeth, who had cared for his ailing mother. She invited him to her home if he was ever in the vicinity. This seemed like more than a coincidence — he would be traveling right past her house. He was a bit unsure about stirring up those painful memories of losing his mother, but decided to stop and thank her for her care. The Catletts were excited to see him and invited him to spend Christmas there. John became **enamored** with their oldest daughter Mary, and felt she might just be the woman he would one day marry. Mary's younger siblings delighted to hear John's stories about life at sea, and it was a very pleasant time. John realized he had missed the blessing of a family who loved him. He wondered, had his mother lived, if he would be at the university by now. John stayed for three weeks but, in so doing, lost his chance to catch the ship.

overseer: an agent employed by slaveholders to supervise the daily affairs on a plantation
enamored: to have strong feelings of admiration and love

Kidnapped

> **press-gang:** men sent ashore by naval officers from Royal Navy warships to kidnap British citizens to serve on the ship
>
> **impress:** force
>
> **abducted:** kidnapped, captured
>
> **midshipman:** an officer of the lowest rank

John's father was relieved that he was still alive when he returned, but angry that he had missed his significant opportunity. As a punishment, he signed John up as a crew member on a ship sailing for the Mediterranean. Life as a sailor, but not on his father's ship, was brutal and crude. John thought a lot about Mary and his future. The voyage lasted 11 months. When he returned home, he went to visit her again. He wanted to share with her the deep feelings he had for her but felt the time was not quite right.

On March 1, 1774, John was walking along the Medway River that wound around Chatham. Suddenly, two men came alongside him and dragged him away. They were a **press-gang** rounding up strong men to serve in the Royal Navy. The Royal Navy had the legal right to **impress** men to serve on their ships in times of war, and a war was looming between France and England. John's father tried to get him released, but the British Navy especially wanted men who were experienced sailors. The next day, John and the other unfortunate men who had been **abducted** were taken to the ship, *HMS Harwick*. John learned that many of the crew members were criminals who had been sentenced to work on ships instead of going to prison. John was given the rank of able **midshipman** because of his experience.

Bad Influences

atheist: a person who does not believe in the existence of God

cajoling: coaxing with gentle persuasion or false promises

blasphemies: shows of contempt for God

The gunner on the *Harwick* befriended John, but it proved to be an unprofitable relationship. The gunner was an **atheist**. He was determined to make John into one, too. Because of this man's **cajoling**, John began to doubt his lifelong belief in God. He started reading a book by an influential atheist, and he and the gunner often discussed the ideas the author presented. Sadly, John soon turned his back on God and the Bible. He made up stories to mock the Bible and twisted Scripture. He entertained the crew with such **blasphemies**.

One day during a time when the *Harwick* was in port, John asked permission to leave the ship for a few days to visit Mary, the woman he desired to marry. After all, it would be five years before the ship

returned and he would see her again. The captain granted him permission but specified he must not be tardy returning. John promised, rented a horse, and rode to the Catlett's house. They welcomed him warmly again. He told Mary he would be gone for five years and asked her to wait for him. She said she could not promise, but she did promise to write. Time passed, and John stayed with the family for a week. He dreaded facing the captain on his return. The captain exclaimed, "John, this is the last time I will trust you. I have no respect for men of such low caliber."[31]

John Flees and Is Caught

Shortly after the *Harwick's* departure, a bad storm damaged the ship. They had to anchor at Plymouth to repair damages. While there, John heard that his father was in Tor-Bay. He had invested in some ships and now owned an interest in an African company that traded in slaves. John began to scheme that if he could get off this Royal Navy ship, just maybe his father would get him a job on his ship *The African*. One day, the captain sent John to check on some of the men who had gone ashore. He wanted to be sure they did not plan to desert, which happened often with men who had been pressed into service. Here was the chance John had been longing for. He walked for a few days when suddenly he was approached by some soldiers looking for him. The captain had discovered that he had deserted.

Then things got really hard for John. The captain, disgusted with his behavior, had him put in **irons** and thrust into the dark, damp prison room of the ship. In a couple of days, the captain had him stripped to the waist, and he was lashed 100 times. He was carried

irons: shackles, chains

to the room where wounded soldiers were treated. There a doctor tended to his wounds. When he had recovered, he had to face the second part of his punishment. He was dishonorably removed from his officer's rank and **consigned** to live among the common sailors. He was mocked by the sailors, whom he had sometimes treated poorly while a midshipman. He was angry at the captain; he was miserable; but he did not turn his thoughts to God at all.

During this awful time, John happened to go up on deck and saw a small boat tied up to the ship. He learned that a **Guinea ship** was anchored nearby to make an exchange of men, which was a common practice. Two men from the Guinea ship were being exchanged for two men from the *Harwick*. John begged the captain to allow him to be one of the men exchanged. The captain agreed, probably glad to be rid of John and his troublemaking. Years later, John acknowledged that this was an act of God's **providence** on his behalf.

In 1745, John became very ill and had to stay in West Africa with Amos Clowe, a slave dealer. Clowe left Newton with his wife, Princess Peye of the Sherbro people, when he set off on another trip. According to Newton, she abused and mistreated him just as much as she did her other slaves.

Eventually John was rescued by the captain of the ship *Greyhound*. The *Greyhound* was a cargo ship owned by John's father's friend, Joseph Manesty. It was headed back to England. During his time on board as a passenger, John began reading a book by a German priest named Thomas à Kempis entitled

consigned: sent

Guinea ship: a boat owned by the Guinea Company, which evolved into England's first slave-trading company

providence: divine intervention

The Imitation of Christ. He wrote, "True peace of heart can be found only by resisting the passions, and not by yielding to them. Consider then how miserable thou makest thyself by placing thy confidence or the joy in any other save the sweet Friendship and Company of Jesus."[32] These thoughts made John search his own heart. What if they were true? He had definitely been giving in to his base passions. He began to remember the Bible verses and hymns his mother had taught him. His heart was stirred.

Salvation in the Storm

One night during the trip, they encountered a terrible storm. John heard sailors yelling that the ship was sinking. All hands were needed on deck. As he scrambled up to the deck, he was horrified to see a sailor get washed overboard to his death. John made his way to the pumps in a last-ditch effort to help correct the situation. Realizing that the ship could sink, John blurted out, "If this will not do, the Lord have mercy on us."[33] He even surprised himself in crying out to God for mercy. John Newton, while **lashed** to the helm on deck, saw his life pass before him. He remembered his dear mother teaching him passages from the Bible and songs from Isaac Watts' hymnal for children. He remembered the many times God had protected his life from near death. His soul was struggling with conviction over his sin. He remembered verses he had learned from the Book of Proverbs. He resolved that if God would spare him from this terrible storm, he would read the New Testament again to see if God would grant him mercy.

The storm did **subside**, and John did read the New Testament. He read

lashed: tied so the storm would not wash him overboard

subside: become gradually less intense

Luke:11:3: “If ye then, being evil, know how to give good gifts to your children; how much more shall your heavenly Father give the Holy Spirit to them that ask him?” John Newton wrote that on that day, March 10, 1748, “The Lord came from on high and delivered me out of deep waters.”[34] He realized that he could find forgiveness at the Cross of Christ. When Christ bore the sins of the world, that included the sins of wicked sailors like himself. He later wrote the hymn, “Looking at the Cross,” to explain the change in his life. The final verse of that song says, “With pleasing grief and mournful joy, My spirit now is filled; That I should such a life destroy, Yet live by Him I killed.”[35] This means he marveled that his sin was borne by Christ on the Cross. When the ship finally landed, all the sailors went ashore to the nearest inn to drink and celebrate their safety. John Newton chose to stay onboard in his room, reading the Bible and praying to his God.

John Becomes Captain

When John did go ashore, the first thing he did was attend church — to the shock of his shipmates and captain. He **consecrated** his life to live for the Lord. He later wrote concerning that day: “It was then that I learned to appreciate the obedience of Jesus Christ. I embraced the sublime doctrine of God manifest in the flesh, reconciling the world to Himself.”[36] The second thing he did was to go see Mary. John renewed his relationship with Mary, and the couple was married on February 1, 1750. John was 24 years old, and Mary 21.

consecrated: dedicated

Once more John found himself needing employment. Joseph Manesty again offered him a job — this time as captain of a slave ship, *The Duke of Argyle*.

Although he hated to leave Mary to go to sea, he knew he had to provide for his family. Little did he expect the trouble ahead. His crew threatened **mutiny** on multiple occasions, and 20 of the slaves broke free and tried to overpower the crew. They also tried to poison the drinking water. John began to implement changes on his ship. He started conducting Sunday services and promoted kind treatment of the slaves. He spent hours in prayer, begging God for protection. He wrote to Mary every day.

mutiny: rebellion against authority

By August 17, 1754, the end of his third sea trip, John started to dread leaving Mary. He also began to develop a growing concern about being involved in the slave trade. It was considered a noble profession by most people at this time in England, but John was beginning to think differently because he was reading the Bible. He returned home to Chatham. He enjoyed time with his wife but realized he needed to have more income since funds were growing low. His distaste for the slave trade grew, and he secretly prayed, "God, please find me some other employment."[37] That answer to his prayer was to come soon.

A Life Change

In early November, he and Mary were enjoying a cup of tea. He was preparing to head off again as captain of the ship *The Bee*, bound for Africa. John suddenly fell to the floor of his house, unconscious. He soon awoke, still dizzy, and his head ached. Mary called for the doctor who declared him unfit for the rigorous life of a sailor. John remarkably recovered but never went back to sea. He later said God had intervened for him yet again through that incident which changed his life forever.

John spent much time with the Lord in the Word. He also had the opportunity to hear George Whitefield preach each morning at his tabernacle. John described the experience: "Rose at 4 and after private prayer went to ye Tabernacle … and here I had a blessing; there were about 1,000 or more people of different persuasions, but all agreed in ye great essentials of ye Gospel and in mutual charity, worshipping the Lord with one heart and soul. Never before had I such an idea and foretaste of ye business in heaven … we were about 3 hours in ye ordinance, at the end I went away rejoicing."[38]

John read all the written works of Whitefield and Wesley, and decided that God wanted him to share the Gospel with others.

John needed a job to support his family. Joseph Manesty again came to his rescue and offered him a job as Tide Surveyor. John was responsible for checking incoming ships for illegal items that were often smuggled in. He enjoyed his job, which had the advantage of leaving him time for ministry. In September 1755, he heard Whitefield preach at several open-air meetings. He and Whitefield became good friends.

John and Mary made a commitment "to declare God's goodness together, not merely in secret or to each other, but by the whole course of our lives; to love Him more than we love each other; and to commit to Him our dearest concerns, and in every trouble to go to Him who has so often heard our prayers and done us good."[39]

John Begins to Preach

John and Mary attended many revival meetings in Yorkshire where John began to have opportunities to share his testimony. People flocked to hear his experience as a former slave trader who found God's grace. A friend encouraged him to write about his life and God's faithfulness to him amid all the trials as a sea captain.

As he gained more confidence in speaking, he was asked to become a full-time minister of the Gospel. On his 37th birthday, he spent the day in prayer and fasting to hear from the Lord. He accepted the call to pastor at the parish church of St. Peter and St. Paul at Olney in Buckinghamshire. He wrote to Mary, "I now almost stagger at the prospect before me. I am to stand in a very public point of view, to take the charge of a large parish, to answer the incessant demands of stated and occasional services, to preach what I ought and to be what I preach. Oh, what zeal, patience, watchfulness will be needful for my support and guidance. My only hope is in the name and power of Jesus Christ."[40]

The Church at Olney

John settled into a routine of rising at 5 a.m. to pray and read the Bible for two hours. He described this practice as: "The one is the fountain of living water and the other the bucket with which we are to draw it out."[41] After breakfast he wrote letters and sermon notes. During the afternoons he walked around the town meeting the people, having conversations, and getting to know their needs and concerns. His sermons then would be planned to answer the questions they were asking. Within weeks, the congregation began to grow. If people walked more than six

miles to attend, he invited them to dinner before they set out for home.

Shortly after the Newtons arrived at Olney, the book he had written about his experiences was published. He prayed that people who read it would experience God's forgiveness as he had. Much to his surprise, the book served to make him famous. On Sundays, people came from as far away as London to hear him preach. Sometimes he preached 12 sermons in a week.

John and Mary both loved children and held special meetings for them, teaching them to love God. He taught the children hymns and Scriptures that his mother had taught him many years before. They frequently had as many as 200 children attending.

It was at Olney that John first met **William Cowper**. The two developed a close friendship. John had begun holding **"cottage meetings"** and Cowper helped him write hymns that would reach the hearts of attendees. They eventually compiled a hymnal called *The Olney Hymnal*. It consisted of 280 songs written by John Newton and 68 by William Cowper. Thousands of hymnals were published and distributed throughout England and the American colonies.

In December 1772, John was reading back through one of his journal entries from the past. He was struck by how much he had grown and how God had seen him through many trials. He needed to write a hymn for the New Year's Eve service to accompany a message on 1 Chronicles 17, which was a humble prayer by King David. He gave the hymn the title, "Faith's Review and Expectation." He intended to illustrate how God

William Cowper: an 18th century English poet and Anglican Hymnwriter

cottage meetings: meetings in homes

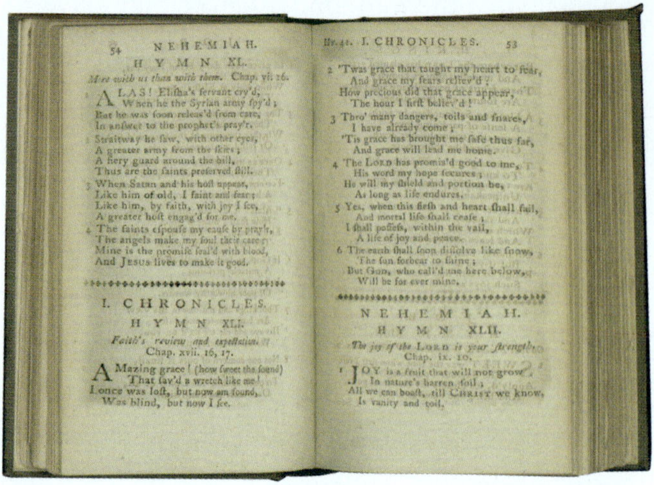

54 NEHEMIAH.

HYMN XL.

More with us than with them. Chap. vi. 16.

1 ALAS! Eliſha's ſervant cry'd,
When he the Syrian army ſpy'd;
But he was ſoon releas'd from care,
In anſwer to the prophet's pray'r.

2 Straitway he ſaw, with other eyes,
A greater army from the ſkies;
A fiery guard around the hill,
Thus are the ſaints preſerved ſtill.

3 When Satan and his hoſt appear,
Like him of old, I faint and fear;
Like him, by faith, with joy I ſee,
A greater hoſt engag'd for me.

4 The ſaints eſpouſe my cauſe by pray'r,
The angels make my ſoul their care;
Mine is the promiſe ſeal'd with blood,
And JESUS lives to make it good.

I. CHRONICLES.

HYMN XLI.

Faith's review and expectation.
Chap. xvii. 16, 17.

AMazing grace! (how ſweet the ſound)
That ſav'd a wretch like me!
I once was loſt, but now am found,
Was blind, but now I ſee.

Hy. 41. I. CHRONICLES. 53

2 'Twas grace that taught my heart to fear,
And grace my fears reliev'd;
How precious did that grace appear,
The hour I firſt believ'd!

3 Thro' many dangers, toils and ſnares,
I have already come;
'Tis grace has brought me ſafe thus far,
And grace will lead me home.

4 The LORD has promis'd good to me,
His word my hope ſecures;
He will my ſhield and portion be,
As long as life endures.

5 Yes, when this fleſh and heart ſhall fail,
And mortal life ſhall ceaſe;
I ſhall poſſeſs, within the vail,
A life of joy and peace.

6 The earth ſhall ſoon diſſolve like ſnow,
The ſun forbear to ſhine;
But GOD, who call'd me here below,
Will be for ever mine.

NEHEMIAH.

HYMN XLII.

The joy of the LORD *is your ſtrength.*
Chap. ix. 10.

1 JOY is a fruit that will not grow
In nature's barren ſoil;
All we can boaſt, till CHRIST we know,
Is vanity and toil.

had led him so far in his life, with the expectation that he would continue to guide him in the future. He picked up his pen and began to write:

> "Amazing grace, how sweet the sound
> That saved a wretch like me
> I once was lost but now am found
> Was blind but now I see."

Over the next few days, he added five more verses to the hymn.

The new hymn was sung at the Olney church on New Year's Day. "The words found their enduring musical companion in America around 1835. Joined to a popular folk tune, 'Amazing Grace' became a favorite song in the revivals sweeping the United States in that century."[42] It is still a favorite today and has blessed countless millions. Today, it is the most popular hymn in the English language and is sung over 10 million times a year in churches and many other venues.

Another Move

prestigious: well-known

Soon after the second printing of the hymnal, John received a letter from his friend John Thornton. "My good man, you have done very well at Olney and are loved and known all over England. Now I have a proposition for you. Several congregations have combined with St. Mary's of Woolnoth in London and are looking for a pastor. Would you consider it?"[43] John was now 54 years old. He never expected an invitation from such a **prestigious** church. After praying about it, John accepted and moved his family there. His reputation had preceded him, and the church was soon full of people coming to hear him preach. John continued writing hymns to coordinate with his sermons. In 1779, shortly after moving to London, he penned the beloved hymn "Glorious Things of Thee Are Spoken."

In December 1785, John received a letter from William Wilberforce, a young member of Parliament. He wanted to learn how to become a Christian. He also asked John to help him take up the fight for the abolition of slavery in Parliament. To see slavery abolished had been a burning desire for John now for many years. Britain had made it illegal for a British citizen to own a slave in 1772, but England still remained the biggest slave-trading nation in the world. It seemed the entire British nation was in some way dependent on the income from the trade. "Thousands of people from members of the royal family to bishops in the Church of England, grew rich from the slave trade."[44]

John wanted to do anything he could to help William champion the abolition movement. John had first-hand knowledge of its evils, and he felt compelled to speak out on behalf of the slaves. John, now 62 years old, wrote a booklet entitled, *Thoughts Upon the African*

Slave Trade, which was published in January 1788. He described in detail the terrible conditions on the slave ships. Over 5,000 copies were sold. Each member of Parliament was given a copy. William Pitt, the British Prime Minister, asked John to testify in Parliament. John asked William Cowper to write a poem challenging people to think of slaves as people with feelings. William Wilberforce introduced a bill in Parliament to abolish the slave trade in April 1791. It was defeated by a vote of 163-88. Four years later he introduced the bill again and it was defeated by only 17 votes. John encouraged William to keep up the fight. On February 25, 1807, a bill finally passed both houses of Parliament which made it illegal for any British citizen to engage in the slave trade.

The Final Years

In 1789, John's beloved Mary died of cancer. John was devastated but threw himself into the work of the Gospel. In January 1806, John was still preaching regularly. When he grew mostly blind and almost deaf, a friend asked if maybe he thought it was time to stop preaching. He responded, "I cannot stop! What! Shall the old

African blasphemer stop while he can speak?"[45] His final sermon preached was in October of 1806. Later that year he told an old friend, "My memory is nearly gone, but I can remember two things: That I am a great sinner and that Christ is a great Savior."[46]

John Newton died on December 21, 1807, at the age of 82. He and Mary are both buried in the churchyard of St. Peter and St. Paul in Olney. Inside the church is a series of three stained glass windows. "Flanked by the images of two slave ships is a window showing John Newton preaching from a pulpit. Inscribed beneath it are the words 'Amazing Grace! How sweet the sound.' "[47]

4

William Cowper

Troubled Hymnwriter

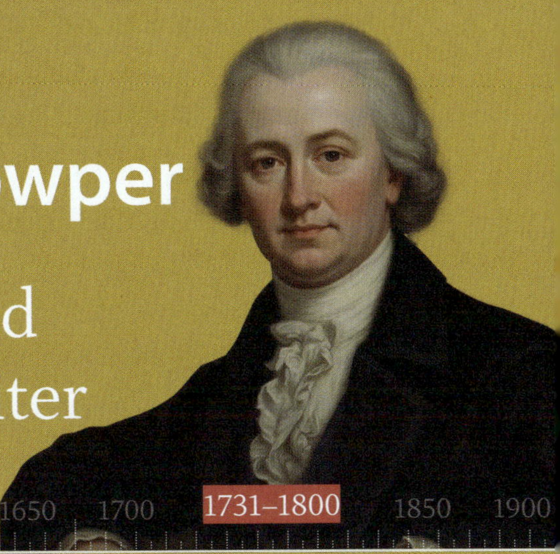

.D. 1450 1500 1550 1600 1650 1700 **1731–1800** 1850 1900

"Then in a nobler, sweeter song, I'll sing thy power to save..."

Hymn: "There is a Fountain"

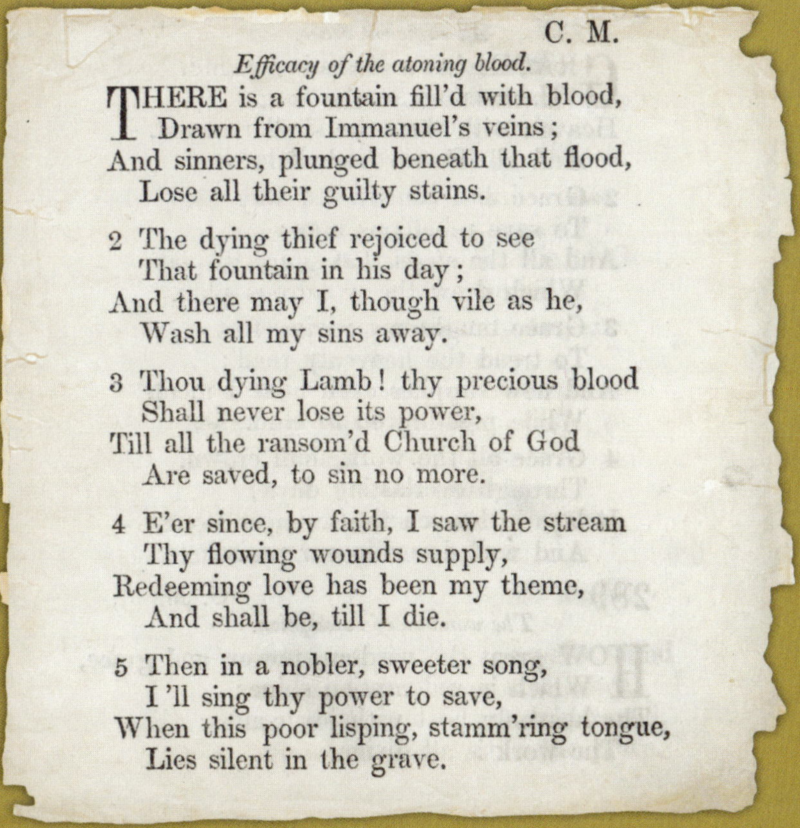

C. M.

Efficacy of the atoning blood.

THERE is a fountain fill'd with blood,
Drawn from Immanuel's veins;
And sinners, plunged beneath that flood,
Lose all their guilty stains.

2 The dying thief rejoiced to see
That fountain in his day;
And there may I, though vile as he,
Wash all my sins away.

3 Thou dying Lamb! thy precious blood
Shall never lose its power,
Till all the ransom'd Church of God
Are saved, to sin no more.

4 E'er since, by faith, I saw the stream
Thy flowing wounds supply,
Redeeming love has been my theme,
And shall be, till I die.

5 Then in a nobler, sweeter song,
I'll sing thy power to save,
When this poor lisping, stamm'ring tongue,
Lies silent in the grave.

Who Was William Cowper?

> **Anglican:** Church of England

William Cowper (pronounced Cooper) was an English poet and **Anglican** Hymnwriter. He was known for writing poetry that reflected everyday life. He had a gift for helping one visualize the English countryside. Even more important than his poetry, he left the world with some of the most loved hymns that have blessed generations of Christians. His most beloved hymn is "There is a Fountain Filled with Blood." He also wrote "God Moves in a Mysterious Way" and "Oh, For a Closer Walk with Thee."

Early Years

William Cowper was born on November 15, 1731, in Great Berkhamstead, Hertfordshire, England. His father was Reverend John Cowper, chaplain to King George II. His mother was the former Anne Donne, a descendant of an English poet. Anne had given birth to three other children, none of whom survived. As she cuddled baby William, she whispered, "May you grow to love God all your life."[48] William adored his mother. As an adult he had no memory of receiving any training in the Bible while young. The only thing he remembered pertaining to religion was that "as a child, he would see the people at 4 o'clock in the morning coming to hear Whitefield preach in the open air."[49] Sadly, when William was only five years old, his mother died while giving birth to his brother, John. William could not stop crying. He was heartbroken. His stern father could not deal with William's grief and sent him away to boarding school at age six.

Living in Fear

The boarding school was a chilly, gloomy building. Here, William spent two miserable years with boys quite a bit older than himself. There was one 15-year-old boy in particular who tormented him and some of the other small boys. This boy threatened him not to tell the authorities. William later wrote, "I well remember being afraid to lift my eyes upon him higher than his knees .... I knew him by his shoe-buckles better than any other part of his dress."[50] William never mentioned his name but only called him "The Boy" who locked him in dark, damp cellars, held his head in rain barrels, and stood lurking over his bed at night. William lived in terror of the boy who threatened to kill him if he ever told anyone. This experience affected William for his entire life.

One day, however, the headmaster caught this boy in the act of tormenting other boys. He **summoned** possible victims into his office to inquire about the boy's actions. William was too fearful to answer the headmaster's questions. Still, the man ascertained by the wild look of fear in the boy's eyes that William was one of his victims. The boy was called into account, finally confessed, and was **expelled** from school. William was relieved but continued to fear that the boy might someday return.

summoned: called

expelled: sent away

Soon after this, William developed a severe eye infection, and his father sent him to live with a famous London eye doctor. For two years, William remained there. At age 10, he was enrolled in Westminster School. William had a gift for writing poetry and did well with his studies. He learned French, Latin, and Greek so well that 50 years later, he translated Homer from Greek to English. When he turned 18, he returned home for nine months, the longest period he spent there since his mother died.

Studying Law

anonymously: without identifying the source

disheartening: losing hope, spirit, or morale

William's father decided to apprentice him to Mr. Chapman, solicitor of Ely Place, Holdon, to study law for three years. This was one of the happiest times of his life, although he hated the study of law. Here, he won the love of everyone around him "by the gentleness of his manners, and amiable temper."[51]

During this time, William and his friend Edward Thurlow spent many happy hours at the home of William's uncle Ashley Cowper. Between 1749 and 1756, he regularly visited his uncle's family on the weekends. He fell in love with his cousin Theodora. The relationship blossomed during the seven years, but then, for some reason, his uncle forbade the couple to marry or even see one another. William was crushed but followed his uncle's wishes. The couple never saw each other again. However, Theodora followed William's career and **anonymously** contributed money during his times of financial need. Neither William nor Theodora ever married. William wrote 19 poems to her during the time they were together. Shortly after this **disheartening** time, William's good friend Sir William Russell drowned in the Thames River.

Looming Depression

House of Lords: the upper chamber of Parliament

William had faced so many disappointments in life! As yet, he was not a Christian. He began struggling with times of deep depression. He wrote a poem concerning the loss of Theodora's company and the death of his friend: "Still, still I mourn with each returning day, him snatch'd by fate in early youth away; And her — through tedious years of doubt and pain. Fixed in her choice and faithful — but in vain!"[52]

Later that year, William's father died. Even though he had never been close to his father, William struggled with depression from all his losses. When William was 31, he was recommended for a higher position in the **House of Lords** as clerk of the Journals. This gave him a glimmer of hope. He told his friends, "Perhaps my fortunes are changing."[53]

Much to his dismay, however, some members of the House of Lords insisted he be given an oral examination at the Bar of the House to assure his suitability for the job. In preparation, he studied the Journals for six months. He later wrote, "I read without perception, for almost half a year altogether. My feelings were those of a man when he arrives at the place of execution."[54]

William was painfully shy. The thought of the examination so disturbed him that he attempted suicide as an answer to his dilemma. He later recalled a strange incident. "I well recollect when I was about 11 years of age, my father desired me to read a vindication of self-murder and give him my sentiments upon the question: I did so and argued against it. My father heard my reasons, and was silent, neither approving nor disapproving; from whence I inferred that he sided with the author against me."[55]

His suicide attempt was unsuccessful but, of course, he was therefore deemed unfit for the job. William was now convinced that God's wrath was upon him. He was tormented by his own sin. His friends, concerned for William, summoned his brother John who also was not yet a Christian. John feeling inadequate to help, asked their cousin, the Reverend Martin Madan of the Church of England, to come and speak to William. Martin shared the life-giving Gospel with William and explained that all men are born sinners. Christ died to atone for the sins of men on Calvary. At that point, William later confessed that "his heart burned" when he heard this.[56]

When confronted with the invitation to give his life to Christ personally, William only expressed a wish to be able to believe. His mental state **deteriorated**. Concerned for William's welfare, his brother John and cousin Martin Madan consulted on the matter. It was decided to send him to Dr. Cotton's **asylum** in St. Albans. William was very opposed at first but decided if they thought it would really help, he would agree.

deteriorated: grew worse

asylum: an institution offering shelter and support to people who are mentally ill

Collegium Insanorum: College of the Insane

William Enters the Asylum

So, in December 1763, William became a patient of the highly respected Dr. Cotton at the **Collegium Insanorum**, who happened to be a poet himself. He became a friend to William. Dr. Cotton was a born-again Christian, and a copy of the Bible was placed in every room. William had many conversations with the kindly Dr. Cotton. William began to hope that perhaps Christ could extend mercy to him. One day, he picked up a copy of the Bible and opened it to Romans 3:25. He read, "Whom God hath set forth to be a propitiation through faith in His blood, to declare His righteousness for the remission of sins that are past, through the forbearance of God."

William Is Saved

William recounted his conversion in these words: "Immediately I received the strength to believe it, and the full beams of the Sun of Righteousness shone upon me. I saw the sufficiency of the atonement He had made, my pardon sealed in His blood, and all the fullness and completeness of His justification. In a moment I believed and received the Gospel. Whatever my friend Madan had said to me, long before, recurred to me with the clearest evidence of its truth, with the demonstration of the Spirit and with power. Unless the Almighty Arm had been under me, I think I should have

died with gratitude and joy. My eyes filled with tears, and my voice choked with transport; I could only look up to Heaven in silence, overwhelmed with love and wonder!"[57]

William Cowper was at last saved! His sense of fear of judgment was gone. He finally had peace. That was what Dr. Cotton had been praying for, and he was delighted. During the coming months, William began writing poems about his transformation and the wonder of God. "Behold, I Make All Things New" was the first hymn he ever wrote, shortly after his conversion. William was now 34 years old. He spent happy, peaceful days with Dr. Cotton. William began to pray, asking God for direction for his life, deciding he could not stay at the asylum forever.

William Moves

John acquired a rented room for his brother in Huntingdon, Cambridge. There, William began attending church, where he met a wonderful family with whom he remained friends for the rest of his life. One Sunday, William Unwin, noticing a newcomer to church, invited William to join his family for afternoon tea. It was a delightful time, and they extended the invitation for Sunday dinner. There were four members of the family — Reverend Morley Unwin, the local parish minister, his intelligent and kind wife Mary, their 21-year-old son William, and his 18-year-old sister Susanna. William delighted the family with stories about his salvation, his love for the Lord, and his poetry.

On November 11, 1765, the Unwins invited William to live in their home as a paying guest. William was **exuberant**. He spent time reading,

exuberant: joyfully enthusiastic

gardening, taking long walks through the countryside, and playing **battledore** with the family on pleasant days.

battledore: a game played with a shuttlecock and rackets, a forerunner of badminton

filial: due from a son

Spiritual matters were a priority for the Unwins. They gathered daily to read the Bible and discussed books they were reading. One of the books they were studying was *An Authoritative Narrative* by the famous John Newton, whom they all longed to meet one day. They spent time together daily, singing hymns from *Psalms and Hymns* composed by Isaac Watts and Charles Wesley. William wrote to his aunt, "I need not tell you that a life such as this is consistent with the utmost cheerfulness. Accordingly, we are all happy and dwell together in unity, as brethren. Mrs. Unwin has almost a maternal affection for me, and I have something like a **filial** one for her, and her son and I are brothers. Blessed be the God of my Salvation for such companions …."[58]

William Meets John Newton

In June 1767, tragedy struck the Unwins. Reverend Morley Unwin fell from a horse and died. John Newton was pastor at the church in Olney, Buckinghamshire, England, not far from the Unwins. He heard of their loss and came to visit them. He was such an encouragement to all of them that Mary decided they would move to Olney to sit under his ministry. William moved with the Unwins; he lived with them for the remainder of his life. William wrote of Newton, "A sincerer or more affectionate friend no man ever had."[59] Newton remained William's friend for life. They often took walks together and discussed things of the Lord.

Describing his new location, William wrote: "Olney is a populous place inhabited chiefly by the half-starved and ragged of the earth."[60] The town had 2,000 inhabitants, most of them lace makers who worked 10 to 12 hours a day. Their children were left to roam the streets and care for themselves, fighting, stealing, and destroying property.

John Newton had a friend who provided funds yearly to purchase

food and clothing for the children. He got William involved in helping the children. The children loved William. They would see him coming and cry, "Squire Cowper comes! The Squire is here!"[61] They would run to give William hugs as he brought bread, candles, and blankets to keep them warm. He prayed with the children and their parents and read Scripture to them.

William was still plagued by bouts of depression but said he never felt happier than when he was visiting the poor, sick, and dying to bring them hope in Christ. "Later John Newton would write he never saw a man more dedicated to loving and serving others than William Cowper."[62]

William Pursues New Interests

William became interested in carpentry and developed his skills in building birdhouses, squirrel houses, and rabbit cages. He had always loved animals. William kept many pets, including dogs, cats, and rabbits which he doted on. He used his newly acquired **proficiency** to build beautiful tables and stools.

Always a lover of nature, William began to paint landscapes to illustrate God's handiwork in the beauty around him. He enjoyed gardening both with flowers and vegetables. He even tried his hand at growing some melons, cucumbers, and pineapples, which were not **native** where he lived. These activities helped to **stem** the waves of depression he sometimes experienced.

William's next-door neighbor, Thomas Aspray, allowed William to write in a summer house on his property. William called the cozy retreat his "verse manufactory" because he often would go there to write poetry or compose hymns. The door of the little building opened onto the garden, which was full of sweet-smelling roses, pinks, and honeysuckles. Here,

proficiency: skill

native: normally grow

stem: restrain

enhance: improve, make memorable

William would sit and write hundreds of poems and hymns as well as many letters to his friends and cousins. John Newton was a frequent guest at the summerhouse. He and William would discuss the text for Newton's sermons. They would develop ideas for hymns to **enhance** the lessons.

William had the pleasure of leading his brother John to the Lord a few days before John died in March of 1770. Moments before he passed away, John praised God and told William, "I am as happy as a King!"[63] William was terribly sad but nevertheless greatly comforted that his brother was now in heaven.

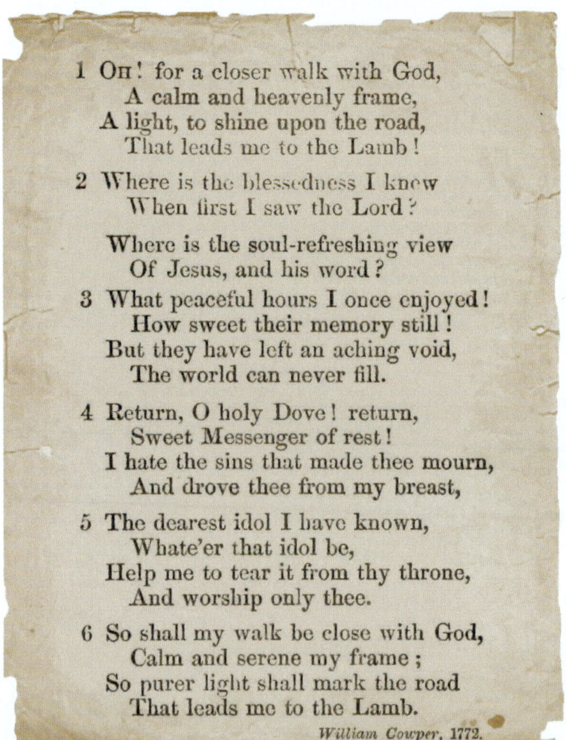

1 Oh! for a closer walk with God,
A calm and heavenly frame,
A light, to shine upon the road,
That leads me to the Lamb!

2 Where is the blessedness I knew
When first I saw the Lord?
Where is the soul-refreshing view
Of Jesus, and his word?

3 What peaceful hours I once enjoyed!
How sweet their memory still!
But they have left an aching void,
The world can never fill.

4 Return, O holy Dove! return,
Sweet Messenger of rest!
I hate the sins that made thee mourn,
And drove thee from my breast,

5 The dearest idol I have known,
Whate'er that idol be,
Help me to tear it from thy throne,
And worship only thee.

6 So shall my walk be close with God,
Calm and serene my frame;
So purer light shall mark the road
That leads me to the Lamb.

William Cowper, 1772.

The Olney Hymnal

"The more William studied the Bible with John Newton, the more he wanted to praise God for communicating His thoughts to man."[64] John had the idea of collaborating with William to compile a book of hymns to be sung in his church. He also thought this would be a good project for William to focus on. William was excited about the idea, which would allow him an outlet to communicate his faith to others. During 1772–1773, William wrote 68 hymns, including his most famous, "There is a Fountain." He was inspired to write this hymn from Zechariah 13:1: "In that day there shall be a fountain opened to the house of David and to the inhabitants of Jerusalem for sin and for uncleanness."

NOTE: There are two more verses he wrote that we don't find in our hymnbooks today:

> "Lord, I believe Thou hast prepared (Unworthy tho' I be)
> For me a blood-bought free reward
> A golden harp for me!
> 'Tis strung and tuned, for endless years,
> And formed by power divine;
> To sound in God the Father's ears,
> No other name but Thine."

When *The Olney Hymnal* was finished, Newton had written 200 of the hymns and William contributed 68. Among the hymns William wrote were "O for a Closer Walk with Thee" and "God Moves in Mysterious Ways," the last Olney hymn he ever wrote. *The Olney Hymnal* was published in 1779 and was extremely popular. The original 2,000 copies sold out quickly, and more were printed as Christian churches everywhere wanted copies. Its fame spread to America, and it was reprinted many times.

Final Years

William was encouraged by Mary Unwin to publish a book of his poems. He wrote many poems on religious and moral subjects, which included many Scripture references. Cowper's fame spread with the publication of his writings.

One day in January 1790, a shy young Cambridge undergraduate knocked on Cowper's door. His name was John Johnson. He was a grandson of Roger Donne, who was William's grandfather on his mother's side of the family. John was his second cousin! William was delighted to meet him, and they became close friends. Through William's influence and testimony, John became a dedicated Christian and later a minister of the Gospel. When both William and his dear friend Mary Unwin became old and feeble, John Johnson relocated them to his town where he could care for them.

William wrote his last poem in 1799, and on April 25, 1800, at age 69, he died peacefully in his sleep. John Johnson was with him until the end. William Cowper was at last with his Lord, and we are left with a "legacy of hymns and poetry permeated with his faith in Jesus Christ, words that have endured well over two centuries."[65]

5

Fanny Crosby

Blind Hymnwriter

D. 1550 1600 1650 1700 1750 1800 **1820–1915** 1950 2000

"This is my story, this is my song, Praising my Savior all the day long"

Hymn: "Blessed Assurance"

Who Was Fanny Crosby?

Frances Jane (Fanny) Crosby was the author of over 8,000 hymns and gospel songs The amazing fact is she was blind from the time she was six weeks old. She was also a teacher of blind students and ministered in a rescue mission. She did not let her blindness prevent her from serving. She once said, “I am so glad that the first face I see will be the face of the Lord Jesus.”[66]

The Early Years

Fanny Crosby was born in Southeast, New York, on March 24, 1820. When she was just six weeks old, she developed an infection in her eyes. Her father drove as fast as he could to get to the doctor but was unsuccessful. Instead, he found a man who claimed to be a physician and offered to come look at the baby. As the family watched anxiously, he put hot **poultices** on Fanny’s eyes, explaining that they would draw out the infection. The infection did **dissipate**, but the treatment resulted in thick white scars covering her eyes. Fanny was nearly blind. She could only discern extremely intense light and sometimes various **hues**.

Shockingly, another disaster struck the family in November. Fanny’s father John was working in the fields on a cold, rainy day and came in at night badly chilled. The next day he became seriously ill and died a few days later. Fanny’s mother Mercy had to take a job as a maid for a wealthy family nearby. The care of little Fanny fell to Mercy’s mother Eunice. Grandmother Eunice was one of the biggest blessings in Fanny’s life. She was a woman of strong faith in

poultices: heated, moist material

dissipate: gradually vanish

hues: colors or shades

the Lord. One of her favorite sayings was, "What can't be cured, can be endured."[67]

invalid: disabled, prevented from living a normal life

Happy Childhood

When it became clear that Fanny could not see, Grandmother Eunice resolved that Fanny would not be a helpless **invalid**. She determined that she would be her granddaughter's eyes. Fanny recalled her grandmother "taking me on her knee and rocking me while she told me of the beautiful sun with its sunrise and sunset. My grandmother was more to me than I can ever express by word or pen."[68] Eunice began exercising Fanny's memory, knowing that she would be depending on it all her life. She took Fanny on walks and taught her many things about flowers and trees by handling objects and being aware of their characteristic smells. She taught her different types of bird songs and described what each bird looked like.

Grandmother Eunice also had a tremendous impact on her spiritually. She instilled in Fanny that God is an ever-present help in trouble. Fanny's earliest memories were of Grandmother Eunice reading the Bible to her. She took time to explain every

detail. She rocked Fannie in her favorite rocking chair, telling her of a "kind heavenly father Who sent His only son Jesus Christ down into this world to be a Savior and Friend to all mankind."[69]

Fanny wrote, "She taught me to believe that our Father in heaven will always give us whatever is for our good, and therefore we should be careful not to ask Him anything that is not consistent with His holy will."[70] In the evenings Grandpa would read her poems and exciting stories.

Fanny Visits an Eye Specialist

Mercy saved up money to take Fanny to an eye specialist in New York City. They made the trip a few weeks after Fanny's fifth birthday. Fanny thoroughly enjoyed the trip, first by wagon and then by boat on the Hudson River. The eye exam was long and thorough, but unfortunately, the doctor said there was nothing they could do. Mercy was crushed, but Fanny remembers thinking whatever sight was, she must not need it. She wrote a poem to express how she felt:

> "Oh, what a happy soul I am,
> Although I cannot see,
> I am resolved that in this world,
> Contented I will be.
> How many blessings I enjoy
> That other people don't!
> To weep and sigh because I'm blind
> I cannot nor I won't."[71]

Mercy struggled with the diagnosis. Grandmother Eunice reminded her, "Now daughter, if the Lord does not give what you prayed for, then He knows that it is better for you not to have it."[72]

Relocations

That same week, Mercy got a new job as a housekeeper in North Salem, Massachusetts, a predominantly Quaker town. She promised Fanny that Grandmother would visit several times each week. Fanny loved the new village and its people. She made friends easily. Grandmother came to teach her, and by the time Fanny was eight years old, she had learned many sections of the Bible.

When Fanny was nine years old, her mother moved again, this time to Ridgefield, Connecticut. Fanny was left during the day with Mrs. Hawley, the landlady. Mrs. Hawley resolved to teach Fanny as Grandmother had done. She had Fanny memorize chapters of the Bible, sometimes five a week. Fanny had a **phenomenal** memory. After a year, she had memorized Genesis, Exodus, Leviticus, Numbers, and the four Gospels. At the end of two years, she added many Psalms, all of Proverbs, Ruth, and Song of Solomon. Fanny said, "When I want to read something from the Bible, I just turn a little button in my mind and there it is waiting for me."[73] Mrs. Hawley also taught her many practical lessons and read poetry to her. Fanny began attending a Presbyterian church. She joined the singing school for young people. She sometimes attended the Methodist church with a friend and sang the great old hymns of Wesley and Watts.

phenomenal: extraordinary

Desire to Learn

Life was happy except that Fanny had a burning desire to go to school. She wanted to show the world that a blind girl can do things sighted girls can do. During a visit to Grandmother, she poured out her heart and then prayed to God, "Dear Lord, please show me how I can learn like other children."[74] Grandmother wisely reminded her to make her request known to God and they prayed together.

In her autobiography, Fanny said she felt a burden lifted after that prayer and she had an assurance that God would answer. Soon after, in the summer of 1831, Grandmother Eunice became very ill. Fanny went to see her. Grandmother was sitting in that rocking chair where she had held Fanny so many times as a young child. Grandmother gently told her that she was going home to heaven. Fanny began sobbing inconsolably. Grandmother put her arm around Fanny and asked, "Tell me my darling, will you meet Grandma in our Father's house on high?"[75] Fanny hesitated for a moment, unsure of how to answer. She responded that by the grace of God, she would. They bowed their heads and Grandmother prayed for Fanny one last time. She died very soon afterward.

In November 1834, Fanny's mother told her that she had heard about a new school — the New York Institution for the Blind (NYIB). Fanny said it was the happiest day of her life and exclaimed, "O thank God. He has answered my prayer just as I knew he would."[76]

On March 3, 1855, just before her 15th birthday, Fanny left for New York. She was sad to leave her mother, but said she was willing to make any sacrifice to be able to learn. She was warmly welcomed by all the staff and students. A fellow student named Mary showed her around the school and helped her get settled in her room.

variations: differences

Fanny loved the school. She began learning history, philosophy, English grammar, the Bible, and science. All the maps, globes, and books had raised lines so the students could feel the **variations** in texture. Poetry was her favorite subject. Soon her teachers began asking her to write poems for various events. Sometimes the school held exhibits for the public to demonstrate what blind students could learn. Fanny always had a part in reciting poetry.

A Visit from President John Tyler

One day, Superintendent Jones burst into Fanny's room and told her that the President of the United States had unexpectedly come to visit the school. He asked her to quickly write a welcome poem for the president to be presented in 15 minutes. She told him she would do her best. She quickly bowed her head and prayed for God to help her write in a way that would honor this famous man. God blessed her with words that pictured the greatness of America and the man chosen to lead the country. When she delivered her poem to the crowd, the applause was loud and heartfelt.

Fanny remembered as a young child asking God to give her a way to be a blessing to the world despite her blindness. Writing a poem for President Tyler was one way God granted that request. He was the first of many famous people to whom Fanny was able to minister during her lifetime. She met many more presidents including James K. Polk, Martin van Buren, John Quincy Adams, and Grover Cleveland; she became lifelong friends with several of them.

packet boats: designed mainly for domestic mail and freight transport

Tour Group

In the summer of 1842, the school decided to send 20 of their outstanding students to tour central New York State. The purpose was to demonstrate to the public how well blind students could learn. The school administration hoped to persuade families with blind children to educate them at the New York Institution for the Blind. The tour group traveled west by the Erie Canal on mule-driven **packet boats**.

A reception was held in each city along the way. The pupils gave speeches, sang, and talked about their school. Fanny traveled with them for two summers, reciting poetry, playing the harp and

piano, and singing. A mother in Oswego was so impressed by the tour group that she decided to send her blind son, Alexander Van Alstyne, to the school. She introduced him to Fanny and asked Fanny to take good care of him. Little did she expect that years later, Fanny and Alexander would marry.

allocate: give

encore: repeated performance

Fanny the Teacher

That fall, Fanny became a full-time teacher at her school, NYIB, teaching rhetoric, grammar, and Roman and American history. Preparation for her classes took up so much of her time that she often stayed up till 2 a.m. to write poetry. On January 24, 1844, Fanny and 16 others had the opportunity to testify before Congress to persuade them to **allocate** money for NYIB. Fanny recited a 13-stanza poem she had written. The Congressmen exploded with loud applause and asked for an **encore**.

By April, Fanny's first volume of poetry, *The Blind Girl and Other Poems*, was published. She wrote thousands of secular poems for many occasions. She ultimately published four books of her poetry. Proceeds from her books helped to raise money for the school.

Fanny Gets Saved

The question asked by her dear Grandmother Eunice as she lay dying five years earlier, plagued Fanny. She did not have the assurance that she would join Grandma in heaven. She contemplated this question again when the cholera plague hit New York and she saw so much death around her. She had a close friend and fellow teacher, Thomas Camp, who invited her to attend revival meetings at the Broadway Tabernacle.

Although Fanny was a deeply religious person, she began to feel that her literary and social concerns had taken first place in her life. She concluded that she could not be sure of her salvation. During the revival meeting when the congregation began to sing the fifth verse of Isaac Watt's "Alas and Did My Savior Bleed," she was struck by the words of the last verse: "Here, Lord, I give myself away, 'Tis all that I can do." She said suddenly, "My very soul was flooded with celestial light. For the first time, I realized that I had been trying to hold the world in one hand and the Lord in the other."[77] She leaped to her feet crying, "Hallelujah!" This experience on November 20, 1850, marked her total dedication to God, making Christ the Lord of her life.

Grover Cleveland

One morning in 1853, Mr. William Cleveland, who was the head of the literary department, came to Fanny's classroom. He had just hired his brother Grover to teach reading, writing, and arithmetic to younger children. He would also serve as clerk in the office of the new superintendent. However, their father had just died, and Grover was particularly grieved by the loss. He told Fanny he thought she could comfort him. Fanny agreed to do her best. That afternoon she met 16-year-old Grover Cleveland, who would years later become president of the United States. They struck up an enduring friendship. Grover would often visit Fanny and write down poems she dictated to him. He continued doing this for a year. They remained friends for life.

Fanny Leaves the Institution for the Blind

On March 2, 1858, Fanny left the New York Institution for the Blind. She had been a student there for eight years and a teacher for 15. Up to this time, she had not written any hymns. Fanny and Alexander Van Alstyne were married in 1858. Fanny had known Van as a pupil and then as a teacher for 15 years. In her autobiography, she wrote about him: "He was a firm, trustful Christian and a man whose kindly deeds and cheering words will not be forgotten by his many friends. We were happy together many years."[78] They had one child who only lived for a few hours. Fanny was heartbroken but turned to God for comfort.

In 1864, Fanny's pastor asked her to write a short hymn for the New Year's Eve service. He was extremely impressed with her ability. In early January, he suggested she go see his friend William Bradbury, the author of many hymns. Bradbury had been looking for someone who could write hymns. He told her that he had wished to meet her for quite a while and asked her to bring him some of her verses that could be set to music. When she brought them, he exclaimed, "Fanny, I am surprised beyond measure, and now, let me say, that as long as I have a publishing house, you will always have work."[79]

Fanny remained with Mr. Bradbury and his publishing house, Bigelow and Main Company, for more than 40 years. Usually, the music came first, and Fanny would write words to fit. Sometimes, however, she wrote a poem and Bradbury or one of his **colleagues** would write the music appropriate for the hymn. They worked side by side for only four years until Mr. Bradbury became very ill. He called Fanny to his office and told her that he would be going soon to be forever with the Lord. He asked her to remain with the company and take up his lifework of creating hymns.

colleagues: associates

Philip Phillips

Another musician with whom Fanny was acquainted, Philip Phillips, was known nationally for his song services. He performed solos with his rich baritone voice. In 1866, he was preparing a hymnal to be titled *The Singing Pilgrim*, based upon John Bunyan's book, *Pilgrim's Progress*. He asked Fanny to write songs based on thoughts in the book. He would supply the music. He gave her a selection of 75 quotations from the book. Fanny memorized them all and selected 40 that she thought would make good poems. When she had "written" all 40 poems in her head, she dictated them to her secretary. Phillips was amazed at Fanny's incredible memory. Her 40 hymns comprised most of *The Singing Pilgrim*. The songbook became very popular.

Compassion for the Poor

tenement house: a building with apartments on each floor, with a shared entrance stairway access

In 1867 Fanny and Van were living in a **tenement house** among the poor. Most of their neighbors lived without outside ventilation or running water in their rooms. "Fanny wanted to live with the poor as one of them, for she believed part of her mission in life was to them."[80] Fanny insisted on giving away any money she possessed except for basic needs. Her desire was to write hymns that would be understood by common people.

About this time, she met William Howard Doane, a wealthy Cincinnati merchant who had a good voice and was a church soloist. He felt that God wanted him to devote more time to developing sacred hymns. He could write melodies but did not have a gift for writing words. A friend, the Reverend Van Meter, was the director of the Five Points Mission. He asked Doane to write a hymn for the anniversary of the founding of his mission work. Doane agreed to try. He prayed, asking God to send him a poem for the celebration. Hearing a knock on his door, he opened it to find a messenger boy with a note. Fanny had been encouraged by Bradbury's friend Robert Lowry to

send Doane her latest poem. Doane was astounded. This poem made the perfect hymn. It was received enthusiastically. Soon afterward, Doane went to visit Fanny, a meeting which began a friendship that lasted 47 years. Doane provided music for more than 1,000 of Fanny's hymns.

Rescue Mission Work

Fanny began speaking at the Bowery Rescue Mission. One night she said, "If there is a man present who has gone just as far as he can, he is the person with whom I want to shake hands."[81] After the meeting closed, a man came to her who said nobody cared for him. Fanny told him, "You are mistaken for the Lord Jesus cares for you, and others care for you too. Unless I had a deep interest in your soul's welfare, I certainly would not be here talking to you on this subject."[82] After Fanny quoted a few passages of Scripture to him, he asked her if she would promise to be there the next evening. She did, and that night he gave his life to the Lord. Fanny

was convinced that people could be won to the Lord through the kindness of others willing to reach out in love. Fanny went home and, unable to sleep, composed the words for "Rescue the Perishing." Mr. Doane wrote the melody the following day. God used this hymn to lead countless thousands to a saving knowledge of Christ.

Fanny spent more than 30 years ministering in rescue missions. One night in the early spring of 1868, she was speaking at a prison in Manhattan when one poor inmate cried out, "Good Lord, do not pass me by."[83] Returning home that evening, Fanny wrote:

> "Pass me not, O gentle Savior,
> Hear my humble cry:
> While on others Thou art smiling,
> Do not pass me by.
> Savior, Savior,
> Hear my humble cry
> While on others Thou are calling
> Do not pass me by."[84]

She sent the words to Doane who wrote the melody, and the hymn was sung a few days later at the same prison. Many prisoners were converted that night.

Prolific Hymnwriter

On April 30, 1868, Doane sent Fanny a desperate message. He had only 40 minutes before he needed to catch a train for Cincinnati. He told Fanny he had a tune and wanted to see if it "said anything" to her. Upon humming the tune, Fanny clapped her hands and exclaimed, "Why, that says 'Safe in the Arms of Jesus.' "[85] Fanny said she always wrote her best hymns when the music "said" something to her. Within half an hour, she had produced the poem. It was an instant success and soon was being sung all over the country.

From the late 1860s, Fanny's songs dominated the hymnbooks produced by Bigelow and Main Company. In 47 years, Fanny furnished Bigelow and Main with 5,959 hymns, although only 2,000 were published. She often wrote several hymns on a subject and let the composer choose from among them.

In 1873, "Blessed Assurance" was written to a melody composed by Fanny's friend, Mrs. Joseph Knapp. Mrs. Knapp played the tune twice on the piano and then asked Fanny what it said to her. Fanny replied:

> "Blessed assurance, Jesus is mine,
> O what a foretaste of glory divine!
> Heir of salvation, purchase of God,
> Born of His Spirit, washed in His blood:
> This is my story, this is my song,
> Praising my Savior all the day long."[86]

The hymn quickly became a favorite all over the world. An English weekly religious paper told the following account of how soldiers used Fanny's hymn titles as passwords in their greetings and responses: "When one member of Soldier's Christian Association meets a comrade he says, "494" which is the number of "God Be With You Till We Meet Again" in *Sacred Songs and Solos*, the latter replies "500" which is the number for "Blessed Assurance." [87] Many believe "Blessed Assurance" to be Fanny Crosby's most famous hymn.

By the early 1870s, Fanny was considered the queen of Hymnwriters. She had a friendship with **Frances Havergal** (another famous Hymnwriter). The two ladies never met but carried on a sweet correspondence for years. Many of Fanny's hymns were published in a songbook titled *Brightest and Best*. Included in the hymnbook were: "I am Thine, Dear Lord," "All the Way My Savior Leads Me," "Savior, More than Life to Me," "To God Be the Glory," "Praise Him, Praise Him," "Jesus, Keep Me Near the Cross," and "Yes, There Is Pardon for You."

Moody and Sankey

In 1876, Fanny, then 55 years old, was introduced to Dwight Moody and Ira Sankey, his soloist. The two men held astonishingly well-attended revival services. They used many of Fanny's hymns in their services and engaged her to write new ones. Sankey wrote many of the melodies for her poems. Sankey wrote the music for

"Saved by Grace," which has been called, "Fanny's Heart Song":

> "And I shall see Him face to face,
> And tell the story —
> Saved by Grace."[88]

During this time, "Fanny spent several days each week at the offices of Bigelow and Main, was active in Christian work among the poor and prisoners, and often directed evening activities in the tenement houses. She was also receiving many invitations to speak … and was traveling a great deal."[89] As always, Fanny did not allow her blindness to **hinder** her ministry. Once she was asked by a student if she ever wondered what her life would have been like if she were not blind. Smiling she responded, "I would not exchange my life for anything. I am shut away by my blindness from the distractions of the world, and it is not an affliction, but a gift from God."[90] When asked what she considered a hymn to be she explained, "A hymn is the song of the heart addressed to God."[91]

In 1877, Fanny met William Kirkpatrick, a composer and publisher of hymnbooks. She supplied nearly 1,000 hymns for "Kirkie," who became a close friend. She also supplied poems for Ira Sankey for his *Gospel Hymns*, which became a six-volume set within ten years.

hinder: obstruct

The Final Years

Fanny suffered a heart attack when she was 80 years old, but as soon as she recovered, she was traveling again. "Rest is for old people. I believe I would not live a year if my work were to be taken from me," she told her sister.[92]

Fanny was invited by Richard Morse, general secretary of the YMCA's International Committee, to speak at the Young Men's Christian Association where he ministered. The chapter he worked with was dedicated to promoting evangelical Christianity, and the improvement of the spiritual, physical, and mental condition of young railway workers. Fanny accepted and it became something she did often. It was a special blessing to her heart when she learned of the many instances God used her music in others' lives.

One night she was explaining what had inspired her to write "Rescue the Perishing." She had been addressing a group of working men years ago. Toward the end of her talk, she was impressed that some wayward son might be in attendance. She pleaded, "If there is a dear boy here tonight who has perchance wandered away from his mother's home and his mother's teaching, would you please come to me at the end of the service?"[93]

Sure enough, an 18-year-old boy came to her asking if she meant him. He explained that he had promised his mother he would meet her in heaven, but after the life he had lived, he was sure he would not be there. She was able to lead the young man to the Lord that night. He joyfully told her he now had the assurance that he could meet his mother in heaven one day. After the meeting at the YMCA was over, an older man took her hand and said, "Miss Crosby, I was the boy who told you more than 35 years ago that I had wandered from my mother's God. That evening you spoke, I found peace . . . And if we never meet again on earth, we will meet up yonder."[94]

That night Fanny went home and was inspired to write a new hymn:

> "Rescue the perishing,
> Care for the dying,
> Snatch them in pity from sin and the grave
> Weep o'er the erring one,
> Lift up the fallen,
> Tell them of Jesus the mighty to save."[95]

The next day Doane put the hymn to music and that song became a sort of battle cry across the nation for those who worked in missions.

Fanny saw many of her friends pass on to heaven before she did. When Ira Sankey was on his deathbed, Fanny visited him. He asked her to meet him in heaven, telling her he would take her by the hand to the throne of God and say to Him, "And now we see Thee face to face, saved by Thy matchless, boundless grace!" Fanny was told that on the morning he passed away, just before going into a coma, he was singing her song, "Saved by Grace."[96]

Fanny continued to speak and entertain guests until her last day. At age 94, she traveled to Longmeadow, Massachusetts, to speak at an outdoor garden event. She suffered another mild heart attack, and the doctor told her she would not live long. She responded, "When I arrive at my eternal home, they will say, 'Come in, Fanny! Come in!' And meanwhile, I have work to do."[97]

Fanny continued writing hymns for a new hymnbook. She usually worked late into the night and slept late. She was now living with her niece Florence and Florence's husband Henry. On February 12, 1915, Fanny went to bed a bit early. Henry checked in on her before he retired and she assured him all was well. A few hours later, she became ill and went to heaven before the doctor arrived. Violets were Fanny's favorite flower, and at her well-attended funeral, everyone was given a violet to drop into the open casket. The choir sang her hymn "Saved by Grace":

> "Some day the silver cord will break
> And I no more as now shall sing.
> But O the joy when I awake
> Within the palace of the King."[98]

6

Horatio Spafford

"It Is Well with My Soul"

D. 1550 1600 1650 1700 1750 1800 **1820–1915** 1950 2000

"Whatever my lot, Thou hast taught me to say, It is well. It is well with my soul." Hymn: "It is Well with My Soul"

Who Was Horatio Spafford?

Horatio Spafford was a lawyer and an elder at the Fullerton Presbyterian Church in Chicago. He suffered terrible financial loss during the Great Chicago Fire of 1871. In 1873, he faced an even more horrifying loss when his four daughters drowned. Their ship, which was bound for England, was struck by a freighter. He is best known for **penning** the hymn "It Is Well with My Soul." He began to do this while passing over the exact spot where the tragic accident occurred. Millions of people have been inspired by this famous hymn.

Early Years

Horatio Gates Spafford, Jr., was born in Troy, New York, on October 20, 1828. His mother was Elizabeth Clark Hewitt Spafford from New York. His father, Horatio Sr., was an inventor, author, editor, horticulturist, and **entrepreneur** who corresponded with famous people such as Thomas Jefferson, John Adams, and James Madison. The Spafford family was well-known and highly respected.

Horatio's father unexpectedly died from a stroke when Horatio was only two years old. His mother was left to run the business and raise Horatio and his sister Elizabeth. She was a strong, capable woman, and the business **flourished** under her leadership.

Horatio attended New York University School of Law and graduated with honors. After being admitted to the **Bar Association**, Horatio had to

penning: writing the words to

entrepreneur: one who organizes and operates a business

flourished: thrived

Bar Association: an organization of attorneys that certifies a law school graduate as a lawyer decide where to start his law practice. He prayed as always when he had to make an important decision. His classmate and best friend, Henry McDaid, encouraged Horatio to move to Chicago to establish a partnership with him. Chicago, Henry reasoned, was an up-and-coming city. With the Spafford family's excellent reputation among **affluent** society, Henry predicted they would have plenty of clients in a short time. So, in 1856, Horatio and Henry traveled west to Chicago.

affluent: wealthy

prominent: famous

tuberculosis: disease caused by bacteria usually effecting the lungs

Successful Lawyer

Horatio threw himself into his law practice and, as predicted, it became exceptionally prosperous. As his wealth and fame grew, he made many generous contributions to community projects. He became a popular dinner guest in many **prominent** households. He became an elder and Sunday school teacher at the Second Presbyterian Church. Here, he became interested in one of his new students, Anna Larssen, later Americanized to Lawson.

Anna Larssen came to America with her family in 1846. They had immigrated from Norway because her father hoped to find work as a carpenter. Chicago was growing and carpenters were in demand. Anna's mother and brother had died during a cholera epidemic. When her father became ill with **tuberculosis**, he and his son moved away from the city thinking that country air would ease the disease. Anna dreaded the thought of leaving friends she had grown close to. Their neighbors, the Elys, invited Anna to stay in Chicago and live with them. Their daughter Sarah and Anna were best friends — almost like sisters. Anna moved in with the Elys and was extremely happy to be treated like a family member.

Sarah invited Anna to church. She was excited about a new Sunday school teacher, Mr. Spafford. She said, "He is so smart! I can't remember ever enjoying Sunday school as much as I do with Mr. Spafford."[99] Horatio involved his students in discussions, asking them questions to engage their participation. He was quite impressed with Anna's Bible knowledge. That afternoon, Anna told Sarah, "You were right, Sarah. I like Mr. Spafford. He has a way of making you really think about the Bible. I've never heard anyone talk about how the Bible can be used in our daily lives before."[100]

Anna and Horatio continued to be impressed with each other. Anna loved how Horatio was devoted to the Lord and how he inspired his students to live for the Lord. Horatio found Anna to be quick to apply specific verses of Scripture to whatever topic they were discussing. She had read her Bible daily since she first learned to read. As time went by, Horatio knew he had met the love of his life and asked Anna to marry him. However, Horatio was 14 years older than Anna. Anna, Sarah, and the Ely family decided that it would be wise for Anna to finish her education first. She attended the Ferry Institute for Young Ladies,

28 miles from Chicago, for the next three years. Horatio and Anna corresponded during that time and their relationship grew. Finally, in 1861, the couple married. During the next 10 years, they became the parents of four beautiful baby girls. "Horatio had achieved every man's dream: a highly successful career, a loving family, and the respect and admiration of the community."[101]

privileged: enjoying benefits and advantages

Meeting Dwight L. Moody

One day during his lunch break, Horatio stepped outside and heard Dwight L. Moody preaching from the courthouse steps. Moody was explaining what true repentance is: "You see, repentance is deeper than feeling. It is action. It is turning right about. And God commands all men everywhere to turn."[102] Horatio pondered what he had heard all day long. He listened to the evangelist for the next two days. He had repented daily of his sin since he was a boy, but now he realized his passion had been pursuing wealth and power. Moody's preaching that day changed the life of this **privileged** businessman forever. He made the conscious decision to focus more of his attention on ministry than business. He immediately began helping Moody organize noontime prayer and worship meetings for businessmen in the city. "Soon thousands of men spent their lunch hours together on their knees, praying for God's power to change their town."[103]

evangelistic: seeking to convert others to Christianity

benevolent: giving money to those in need

commuter train: passenger rail service that primarily operates within a metropolitan area

Horatio began visiting jails and hospitals. He contributed large sums to **evangelistic** and **benevolent** causes. He became one of Moody's financial supporters. In 1870, along with several other business owners, Horatio signed an agreement to begin paying Moody a regular salary. This enabled Moody to preach full-time. Horatio's friendship with Moody brought him in contact with well-known musicians such as Ira Sankey and Philip Bliss. Horatio and Anna owned a pleasant home situated on 12 acres which they used as a place of ministry. Prayers and songs filled the Spafford home many nights as they entertained guests.

The Chicago Fire

Horatio planned to sell some of his property along Lake Michigan. He thought this would free him to be more involved in spreading the Gospel. To do that, he had to travel to Indiana for a few days. Anna and the girls hated to see him go, but knew he would be back soon. He hugged the girls before climbing into the buggy. Peter, his coachman and handyman, drove him to catch the **commuter train**. Then Peter returned to care for Horatio's family in his absence.

The summer of 1871 had been unusually hot and dry. Anna took the girls, Annie, Maggie, Bessie, and baby Tanetta for a swim in Lake Michigan after dinner to cool off. On the way home, Annie wondered what the strange glow in the sky could be. Anna turned to see large clouds of black smoke and flames rising above the city. Was Chicago burning? Realizing that Horatio was not home, Anna

panicked. What would she do if the wind suddenly began blowing north, threatening the safety of their home? Before putting the girls to bed, she led them in prayer for the people in the city whose lives were in danger.

That night, Anna, Peter, and her three household servants began to make **evacuation plans**, praying they would not need them. They decided that Peter would transport them to the family cabin located well away from the city if the fire came closer.

The next morning, Horatio, reading the headlines in the paper, left his breakfast unfinished and ran to the nearest train station. The ticket salesman could not promise they could get close to Chicago under the circumstances. Horatio boarded along with other frightened passengers. He began to pray. "God, grant that my lovely ones are safe. Anna. Oh, Anna, my girls…."[104]

The train made it as far as the south side of Chicago. Horatio witnessed unspeakable destruction as flames were devouring almost every house he saw. Desperate people were fleeing the

evacuation plans: preparations to flee

exorbitant: excessive, overpriced

looters: those who steal during disasters

acrid: irritatingly pungent smell

singed: slightly burnt or scorched

city in wagons, carts, and buggies. People were frantically searching for family members. Children were wandering around, frightened and lost. Some were screaming. Wealthy homeowners were offering **exorbitant** payments to wagon drivers to haul their furniture and belongings to safety. **Looters** were entering ravaged houses and stealing valuables.

Horatio ran to the only bridge offering escape from the city and access to the road that led home. Hundreds of people were jammed on the bridge, which was already beginning to burn. He stopped several times to help desperate women or children across. He ran on, hoping to outrun the flames. He was having trouble breathing through the **acrid** smoke-filled air but knew he must press on. He must get home to his family.

Home at Last

Finally, Anna and the girls heard a cheer as Horatio stumbled through the door. He was covered in smoke, and his hands were slightly **singed**. He was thankful that his beloved girls were safe, and he was home. The fire had stopped only a few blocks short of their house. His home was jammed with people who had lost their homes. Anna had opened her home as a refuge for needy people. Horatio was exhausted. Anna and the girls got him water and food and led him to a chair to rest.

Two days later, Peter drove Horatio to assess the damage to the city. As he had feared, his beautiful office was destroyed. Hundreds of legal books from his library lay in ashes. The entire business district around his office was destroyed — banks, hotels, theaters, restaurants, churches, the *Chicago Tribune* office—all gone. Horatio had invested all his resources in his business strategy, and now there was nothing left. The Spaffords managed to keep their home although they had to take out a **mortgage**. Their loss was traumatic, but they still had their family. Their hearts broke for so many others who were less fortunate. They both devoted time to Relief and Aid Committees to help relieve the suffering of thousands. Chicago slowly began to rebuild from the ruins.

mortgage: a loan

opted: decided

Need for a Vacation

Anna's health began to suffer. The Great Fire had happened only months after Tanetta's birth, and Anna had thrown all her energies into helping others. The doctor recommended that Horatio take his family on a vacation for a much-needed rest. He decided on Europe as they had friends who lived in France. He knew it would tax their already strained finances, but he must get rest for Anna. He bought tickets on the French ship *SS Ville du Havre*, which was considered the most magnificent ship ever built.

Days before they departed, a businessman offered to buy Horatio's land on Lake Michigan! He had thought no one would want it now, with Chicago in ruins. He **opted** to send Anna and the girls ahead and follow in a few days. Anna's close friend and neighbor, Mrs. Goodwin, decided to go along, with her three children and a young friend, Willy Culver. Horatio rode the train with his family and friends to New York City, where the *Ville du Havre* was docked. They met Reverend Lorriaux, a French pastor who promised to look after the family while en route. Horatio waved and threw kisses as his precious family headed off. He bowed his head and offered a prayer for their safety.

Disaster at Sea

Horatio waited for a telegram assuring him they had arrived safely. It was delayed in arriving. On December 1, 1873, a telegram did arrive, but it was from Wales, not France. The message from Anna was, "Saved alone what shall I do. Mrs. Goodwin children Willie Culver lost. Go with Lorriaux until answer reply Porclain 64 Rue Aboukir Paris Spafford."

Horatio felt as if he had been shot. He paced across the room where his beloved daughters played "princess," where he had read them stories just nights before. He learned that another ship had crashed into *Ville du Havre*, and many lives were lost. Horatio sent Anna

a telegram telling her he was on the way. He made the trip to New York with Mr. Goodwin who had also lost his wife and his children, and their friend Willy.

benumbed: overcome

On the sea journey to France, the ship's captain called Horatio and Mr. Goodwin up on the deck. He said, "I do not wish to cause you unnecessary anguish, gentlemen. But I believe you would want to know. We have calculated our location with great care, and we believe this is where the *Ville du Havre* sank."[105] Horatio thanked the captain and moved, **benumbed** by grief, to the bow of the ship. The bodies of his precious little girls lay three miles down in the cold, dark ocean. With tears streaming down his face, Horatio pulled a piece of paper from his pocket. He began to pour out words from his heart filled with both pain and faith.

"When peace like a river, attendeth my way,
When sorrows like sea billows roll,
Whatever my lot, Thou hast taught me to say,
It is well. It is well with my soul.
Tho' Satan should buffet, tho' trials should come.
Let this blest assurance control,
That Christ hath regarded my helpless estate,
And hath shed His own blood for my soul.
My sin — oh, the bliss of this glorious thought,
My sin, not in part, but the whole
Is nailed to the cross and I bear it no more;
Praise the Lord, praise the Lord, O my soul!
And Lord, haste the day when the faith shall be sight,
The clouds be rolled back as a scroll,
The trump shall resound, and the Lord shall descend —
Even so, it is well with my soul."[106]

The following week, Horatio wrote to a relative about the mixture of grief and hope he felt at that moment: “On Thursday last we passed over the spot where she went down, in mid-ocean, the waters three miles deep. But I do not think of our dear ones there. They are safe, folded, the dear lambs.”[107] He pictured them safe in the arms of Jesus. In 1876, Philip Bliss composed the music to fit the words. The hymn was first published in a songbook produced by Ira Sankey, the songleader for renowned evangelist Dwight Moody. “It Is Well with My Soul” has become one of the most cherished hymns ever written.

Reunited with Anna

Horatio met Anna, and they went to London for a rest. She recounted to him what she knew of the wreck. It had been a lovely day, and Anna had tucked the girls in bed that night. Little Tanetta had sung “In the Sweet By and By” several times before going to sleep. At about 2 a.m. they heard a tremendous noise. She wrapped the girls in blankets and headed to the deck. An iron ship, a Scottish cargo vessel called the *Loch Earn*, had collided with them. It soon became obvious that their ship had broken in two. The night was clear, and no one knew what had caused the crash. The crew members struggled to launch the lifeboats, but the boats had been painted in position, and most were stuck.

Their daughter Maggie had been screaming with fear but quieted and said, “Mama, God will take care of us.”[108] Annie, the oldest, said, “Don’t be afraid. The sea is His, and He made it.”[109] In 12 minutes, the deck collapsed, creating a massive whirlpool, sending 226 people to a watery grave. It wrenched Tanetta from Anna’s arms as she reached out and managed to grab a piece of

Tanetta's nightgown. The swirling waves swept her away again. One passenger attempted to rescue two of the girls and almost made it to the lifeboat. Tragically, the girls lost their grip on their rescuer and slipped beneath the waves. Anna was found by rescuers floating semi-conscious, held afloat by a piece of broken planking. She was taken to land with the other surviving passengers. Anna said at first, she wished she had drowned with her girls, but God somehow assured her that she had been saved for a purpose. He had work for her to do. Anna and Horatio held each other tightly, cried, and prayed.

Home Again

D.L. Moody met with Horatio and Anna in London. He told Anna, "Anna, you must go into my work. You must be so busy helping those who have gone into the depths of despair that you will overcome your own affliction by bringing comfort and salvation to others."[110] Anna agreed and soon they all left for home.

Horatio wrote a few more poems for grieving people that were greatly used to comfort many.

Anna became thoroughly involved in ministering to disadvantaged women. Horatio continued his noontime prayer meetings for businessmen, working with the YMCA, and visiting jails and hospitals. Although his finances had dwindled, he still helped Moody build his new tabernacle in 1876. He wrote a new hymn for its dedication service.

There were several families of friends who had experienced tremendous loss since the time of the Chicago Fire. They joined the Spaffords to help relieve the suffering of others and share the good news of the Gospel. The circle of friends called themselves "The Overcomers."

Horatio and Anna were blessed with a baby boy, Horatio Goertner Spafford, born on November 16, 1876. On March 24, 1878, Bertha Hedges Spafford was born. When little Horatio was four, he and Bertha contracted **scarlet fever**. Sadly, little Horatio died, but Bertha recovered. Horatio wrote another hymn after his son's death. He and Anna did not understand why God allowed another child to be taken to heaven, but they chose to trust in God's goodness. Baby Grace was born on January 18, 1881.

scarlet fever: an infectious bacterial disease especially affecting children

Moving to Israel

Years before, Horatio had met a professor who had sparked his interest in the land of Israel. He had always wished to visit Jerusalem, the land where his Lord had walked. He felt drawn to share the Gospel with God's special people. In 1881, The Overcomers heard of many children in Israel who were suffering from hunger, lack of shelter, and lack of medical attention. They felt they were called to leave their homes in the United States, fund the mission, and minister to these children. They traveled to Jerusalem to set up a mission station, which they called "The American Colony." Anna set up a medical clinic and soup kitchen and held mothers' meetings like the ones she had led in Chicago. Horatio led the group in Sunday services. It did not take them long to make friends. Soon, Horatio and the other men began teaching English in local schools and tutored Arab students. The American Colony attracted people from many backgrounds, Muslims included. "Their Sunday dinner guests might include Islamic clerics or Jewish rabbis, a Russian pilgrim, an English professor, a Spanish priest, or even diplomats from foreign embassies."[111] The colony acquired an excellent reputation for Christian hospitality, charity, and compassion.

Horatio continued to write hymns. He led many people to the Lord, including an 18-year-old Muslim man. The Spaffords ministered there for seven years. In 1888, Horatio contracted malaria and died. He was buried in Mount Zion Cemetery.

Anna, Bertha, and Grace stayed in Israel. The American Colony eventually became "The Spafford Children's Center." It is still in operation today, ministering to the poor and needy in Jerusalem and the West Bank. Anna provided care for hundreds of children until she died in 1923 at the age of 81. After her mother's death, Bertha Spafford Vester carried on the work her parents began. The Spafford family still has a part in the operation of The American Colony Hotel in Jerusalem.

Horatio faced many weighty sorrows — financial loss, the Great Chicago Fire, the death of his precious children — but his trust in the sovereignty of God did not waver. "Although darkness threatened Horatio Gates Spafford at every turn, his heart sang 'It Is Well with My Soul.' Over the years, thousands, even millions of believers in Christ have learned to sing it with him."[112]

7

Frances Ridley Havergal

Sermons in a Song

1836–1879

"Take my will, and make it Thine, It shall be no longer mine."

Hymn: "Take My Life and Let It Be"

Who Was Frances Havergal?

Frances Havergal was an English poet and Hymnwriter. Over 200 of her poems and 50 hymns were published. Her hymns have been called "sermons in song." She also wrote Christian tracts, pamphlets, and books. She never married but devoted her entire life to serving her Savior. Frances believed that every mental power we possess, whether memory, judgment, musical talent, or intellect, "may all be dedicated to Him, sanctified by Him, and used by Him. Whatever He has given, He will use, if we will let Him."[113] When asked how she wrote poetry, she responded, "I believe my King suggests a thought and whispers me a musical line or two, and then I look up and thank Him delightedly and go on with it. That is how the hymns and poems come."[114] Some of her most famous hymns include "Take My Life and Let It Be," "Like a River Glorious," "I Gave My Life for Thee," "Who Is on the Lord's Side," "Lord, Speak to Me," "I Am Trusting Thee, Lord Jesus."

Early Years

Frances Ridley Havergal was born on December 14, 1836, to Reverend William Henry Havergal and his wife Jane. Her father was the pastor of the Astley Rectory in Worcestershire, England. He was an accomplished composer and musician. He was passionate about improving the quality of church music. He imparted that zeal to Frances. He donated his earnings from his published works to missionaries and his church. Frances had two older brothers and three older sisters. Frances was a special joy to her father who suffered a partially debilitating accident seven years before her birth. Her sisters all adored her. Her 19-year-old sister wrote of her, "My recollection of Frances begins with the first day of her life; a pretty little babe even then, and by the time she reached two years of age, with her fair complexion, light curling hair, and bright expression, a prettier child was seldom seen."[115] Frances and her brother Frank, who was seven years older, were lifelong friends. Both shared a love and aptitude for music.

Frances was reading and writing by the time she was three years old. Her mother taught her Bible verses daily and practical skills such as sewing and baking. Frances and her mother visited the poor and sick of the community. Frances remembered carrying buckets of soup to needy folks. She visited families with her father also. Both her father and mother loved and served Jesus Christ. They led their children in Bible studies and prayer. Frances lovingly recalled sitting on her father's lap during family worship and listening to his rich voice as the family sang hymns together.

Questions about Eternity

Frances loved being in the family garden and exploring the woods, fields, and brook around the parsonage. Her faithful companion was Flora, her small brown and white spaniel. Frances wrote many poems as a child. "Her parents' fragrant rose garden, the china blue sky, and truant clouds all spoke to her of her Maker's goodness."[116] She marveled at William Cowper's poetry about nature and longed to be a Christian. Part of her wanted to be good but part of her did not. She prayed very hard that God would change her sinful heart. She wrote, "As for trying to be good, that seemed next to no use; it was like struggling in a quicksand, the more you struggle, the deeper you sink."[117] When bothered by these thoughts, she would attempt to push them out of her mind and take Flora for a walk.

Frances' Mother Dies

When Frances was 11 years old, her mother became quite ill. One day she requested that Frances come to her bedside. She told her daughter that she would not recover on earth. She would go see her Savior soon. "Fanny, you are my youngest and I am concerned most for you, Child. Fanny, dear, pray to God to prepare you for all that He is preparing you to do. And remember nothing but the precious blood of Christ can make you clean and lovely in God's sight."[118] Frances could not believe her mother would not get well. On July 5, 1848, her mother died, and Frances ran to her room and cried inconsolably for hours. When the crying stopped, she got out her pen and paper and resolved to write a tribute to her mother's faith. She wrote:

> "Eye hath not seen, nor ear hath heard,
> Neither can man's heart conceive,
> The blessed things God hath prepared
> For those who love Him and believe."[119]

Avid Learner

Although Frances was an active child, she had a gift for focusing on and remembering what she was taught. When her older siblings were being tutored by their German tutor, she would hide behind the curtain and listen. She soon learned to speak German with more accuracy than her older siblings and begged to be allowed to sit in on their lessons. She even taught Flora German commands. She surprised the German tutor one day as she was wandering in the garden singing hymns in perfect German.

When Frances was 13, she was excited that she would be attending boarding school in Belmont. Mrs. Teed, her instructor, required that all students speak only French. Frances loved studying languages. She learned six languages during her life. Mrs. Teed was a devoted Christian and prayed that each student would find new life in Christ while at the school.

Frances Finds Assurance

Christmas time came and Frances was excited to be spending the holidays at home. Her sister Miriam invited family and friends over to celebrate. Caroline Cooke, one of the guests, was especially warm and friendly. Sitting by the fire in the parlor, Frances felt comfortable enough to confide in Caroline. Teary-eyed, Frances confessed, "I want assurance of forgiveness of my sins above everything."[120] Caroline held her close and asked her if Christ were to come this minute in the clouds and take His redeemed up to heaven, could she not trust Him? Would His promise not be enough for her to commit her soul to Him? Suddenly, it all made sense. Frances found assurance at last. Frances later wrote, "There and then I committed my soul to the Savior, I do not mean to say without any trembling or fear, but I did — and earth and heaven seemed bright from that moment — I did trust the Lord Jesus. For the next few days, my happiness increased. Over and over again, I renewed that giving up my soul to the Savior which had made entrance for the joy."[121] For the first time, church services and Scripture readings came alive. Frances was stunned to find out that her father and Caroline were soon to be married. She was thrilled to welcome Caroline to the family.

Off to a New School

> **severe erysipelas:** an acute bacterial infection causing high fevers
>
> **reconnoitering:** a preliminary survey to gain information

On August 5, 1851, Frances, now 14, left for Powick Court, a small private school near Worcestershire, England, which is located two miles south of the city of Worcester. Frances excelled in her studies. Unfortunately, just before the end of the first term, Fanny was feeling extra tired and her face hurt. By the next morning, her eyes were swollen shut, her head ached terribly, and she was nearly blind. The doctor sent her home to recover. She had "**severe erysipelas**". For many weeks, Frances had to lie still. Her father knew how hard this was for Frances and would come to her room and sing to her. Her sister Maria and Caroline would take turns reading the Bible and singing her favorite hymns. Weeks later she was allowed to get up and her sight returned, but it would be months before she could return to school. When she had recovered sufficiently, her father took the family to Wales for a vacation. They explored the copper mines with a guide and took walks **reconnoitering** the beautiful countryside. Frances basked in the beauty of God's creation and was refreshed.

More Opportunities to Minister

Frances' sister Ellen had married and moved to Ireland. She wrote asking Frances to come to sing for a group of Irish girls who attended her weekly Bible study. Frances was thrilled at the prospect, although she hated leaving her newly acquired Sunday school class. She was received with overwhelming success. One Irish girl was inspired by Frances' devotion to the Lord. She wrote, "May the Lord teach me, even me, to know and love Him so."[122]

Frances plunged into the ministry there until it was time to head home.

Frances' Sunday school students back in Worcester were glad to have Frances return. Frances kept careful records of each of her Sunday school students. She visited them, prayed for them, and was eager to spend time with any who wanted to learn more about Jesus. She was constantly busy writing poems and stories. She gave the money she received from her writing to support the mission work being done in Ireland. Frances became a regular contributor to *Good Words* magazine. They printed her hymn, "I Gave My Life for Thee." Fanny excitedly showed her father the letter and said, "Papa, I think that writing may be a ministry for me after all."[123]

She had written the song not long before her 20th birthday while in Germany with her father. In a pastor friend's study, she noticed a painting of Christ crowned with thorns standing before Pilate. Underneath was the inscription, "This I have done for Thee; what hast thou done for Me?"[124] Drawn to the painting and inspired to write:

> "I gave my life for thee,
> My precious blood I shed
> That thou might'st ransomed be,
> And quickened from the dead
> I gave my life for thee,
> What hast thou given for me?
> I suffered much for thee,
> More than thy tongue can tell,
> Of bitterest agony
> To rescue thee from hell.
> I suffered much for thee,
> What canst thou bear for me?"[125]

Frances Becomes a Tutor

spacious: roomy, large

Frances' sister Miriam and her husband Henry, a successful landowner, invited Frances to Oakhampton in Devon, England, to tutor their two daughters. Frances had often written to her nieces, sending poems she wrote especially for them. The girls were waiting excitedly for her arrival. They had all sorts of fun activities planned — swimming, skating, croquet, chess, and trips to the seashore. Henry announced that he had some plans for her as well. He had arranged for her to meet Dr. William Marshall, conductor of the Kidderminster Philharmonic Orchestra. Very soon, Frances would be singing solos there!

Miriam showed Frances to her **spacious** room which had a writing desk, bookshelves, and a comfortable reading chair. Frances' health was better during this time. She kept up with the energetic girls, enjoying ice skating and many outdoor activities.

Frances rose before the children each day to read her Bible and pray. Any spare moments, even small amounts of time, she filled with study. The girls excelled under Frances' tutelage, but when they turned 12 and 13, they enrolled at boarding school.

In Love with the Alps

Frances' parents relocated to a retirement home in Leamington, England, and Frances moved in to help them in their old age. Frances began writing children's pieces with stories such as *Ben Brightboots*, a tale about the Havergal family cat. It was published in 1869 and sold well. She was also teaching, singing, and leading a study group at the YWCA (Young Women's Christian Association). Frances often suffered bouts of illness. Her family tried to get her to slow down and rest more, but it was almost impossible. Frances had a strong desire to be useful to God.

Frances was invited by one of her nieces to accompany the family on a trip to the Alps. It was the first of several she would make to Switzerland. Frances had been enthralled with the Alps ever since reading a book about them as a girl. The real thing was even more magnificent than she had imagined. Frances loved to slide down the mountains without skis while assuming a squatting or standing position. It was called "glissading." Sometimes groups of tourists would rope themselves together and travel down mountainsides together. Frances preferred to "glissade" alone. When the vacation came to an end, Frances exclaimed to her niece, "The works of the Lord are great, sought out of all them that have pleasure therein" (Psalm 111:2, KJV).

Song Books

Frances was soon off again, this time to London. Her first book of poems, *The Ministry of Songs,* was ready for publication in 1869. Her father understood her excitement. He shared Frances' deep appreciation for music and love of God's creation. He had spent his life serving the Lord by ministering in song just as she longed to do. After her first book was published, Frances' fame spread all over England. She received more than 600 letters in the first month after publication. One of her most famous correspondents was Fanny Crosby. The two never met in person, but Frances wrote a poem in honor of her friend and titled it, "A Seeing Heart."

In London, she met her first publisher who also became her singing teacher, Signor Alberto Randegger, a famous composer. He was

delighted with her poems and made her this offer: "So, you see, my dear, if you will write songs and allow me to set them to music, I believe we may offer a new song book especially for children."[126] He asked her to produce 12 songs by the end of October. Songs seemed to come spilling out of Frances. The book was called *Sacred Songs for Little Singers.* It was produced by the London Publisher to the Queen. Frances dedicated the book to the Queen's youngest daughter. Frances often prayed, "Whatever gift of writing, however small, Lord, may it ever only be for Your use."[127]

More Projects

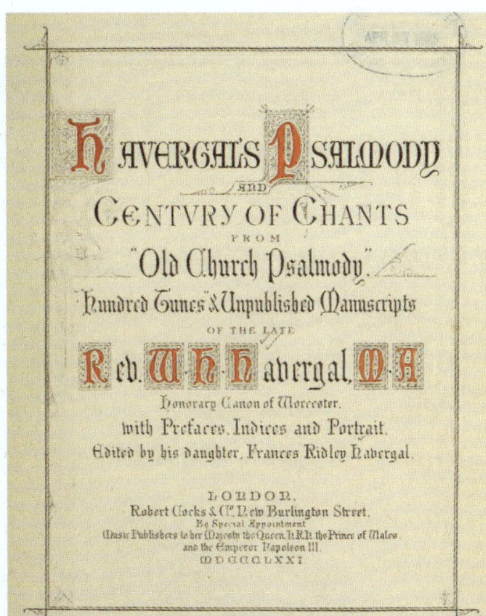

Havergal's Psalmody and Century of Chants from "Old Church Psalmody." "Hundred Tunes" & Unpublished Manuscripts of the late Rev. W. H. Havergal, M.A. Honorary Canon of Worcester, with Prefaces, Indices and Portrait. Edited by his daughter, Frances Ridley Havergal.

London, Robert Cocks & Co. New Burlington Street, By Special Appointment Music Publishers to her Majesty the Queen, H.R.H. the Prince of Wales, and the Emperor Napoleon III. MDCCCLXXI

Frances' father died on Easter Sunday 1870. Frances felt the loss deeply. She began collecting his hymns to have them published and preserved in *Havergal's Psalmody*. Frances wrote several new hymns for Rev. Charles Snepp's *Songs of Grace and Glory*. This collection of hymns was a project she worked on with Rev. Snepp, the editor. She had become friends with his family while vacationing in Switzerland. It was a massive undertaking, but when finished it was considered one of the most comprehensive hymnals in the Church of England. The last song Frances' father wrote just before his death was included in the book. There were many tunes and hymns for every part of the Christian life, and each had to be arranged and cataloged by author and date. Frances often thought about how her father would have loved to be part of the project. She concluded that her skill was due to all he had taught her about music over the years.

Frances was in the habit of asking God for help each time she wrote a new hymn. She had many invitations to sing at large gatherings of people or churches. She continued ministering to young women through the YWCA. She was flooded with editors' requests for her writing, letters of thanks, and people writing to ask her for advice. Her days were full. Her dream of being useful to God was being fulfilled.

Frances' Consecration Hymn

In 1874, she had a financial disappointment. She was expecting a check from her American publisher for her collection of hymns called *The Ministry of Song* as well as an order for her newest book, *Under the Surface*. Instead, she received a letter explaining that he had gone bankrupt.

She wrote to her friend Mr. Snepp about the situation. "I am trusting in His will for me in everything, and learning the wonder of finding myself saying, 'Thy will be done,' not with a sigh, but with a song! All for Jesus really means all, not halfway, and it's so good to put it all in His hands."[128]

Instead of feeling sorry for herself, she focused on the salvation of others. She wrote about visiting a household for five days, where several unconverted family members lived. She was burdened for all ten people in the house. Even those who claimed to be Christians did not seem interested in spiritual matters. Frances explained that she turned to prayer: "Lord, give me all in this house! And He just did! Before I left the house every one had got a blessing. The last night of my visit, after I had retired, the governess asked me to go to the two daughters. They were crying, but then and there both of them trusted and rejoiced; it was nearly midnight. I was too happy to sleep and passed most of the night in praise and renewal of my own consecration, and these little couplets formed themselves and chimed in my heart one after another till they finished with 'Ever, only, ALL for Thee.' "[129]

What Frances entitled "Frances' Consecration Hymn" became the most beloved of all her hymns: "Take My Life and Let It Be."

Frances gave away the majority of her income from her songs to Christian causes. She was frustrated when asked if she could write poetry to fit someone's program. She explained it this way, "No, not unless He gave it to me line by line. The Master has not put a chest of poetic gold into my possession and said, 'Now use it as you like.' But He keeps the gold and gives it me, piece by piece just when He will and as much as He will, and no more."[130]

More Illness

> **typhoid fever:** an infectious bacterial disease contracted from contaminated food or water
>
> **peritonitis:** inflammation of the thin tissue that lines the abdominal wall

Frances had another wonderful vacation in her beloved Alps mountains in 1874. On the way home, she contracted **typhoid fever** and became so ill that her family feared she would die. The doctor forbade her to work for six months. During this time, Frances lived with intense pain. She wrote, "Pain, as to God's own children is, truly and really, only blessings in disguise. It is but His chiseling, one of His graving tools producing the likeness to Jesus for which we long. I never yet came across a suffering (real) Christian who could not thank Him for pain!"[131]

Slowly, Frances' strength began to return. Disregarding the doctor's warning, she began to minister again. She led four Bible classes each week, spoke and sang in mission conferences, answered hundreds of letters, and responded to editors' requests for poems, music, and devotionals. On Christmas Day 1878, Frances became ill once more. While recovering, she continued to keep a journal and worked on her new devotional book, *Kept for the Master's Use*. Always an animal lover, Frances enjoyed playing with her two kittens, Dot and Trot. She received news that the music she had written for *Loving All Along* had been accepted for publication. It was a song that Ira Sankey, a famous singer at D.L. Moody's revival meetings, had requested to take to America for publication. This news delighted her.

Frances continued writing and planning a trip to Ireland in June to minister again. At first, the doctor did not think her illness was serious, but **peritonitis** set in, causing intense pain. Her family kept a close watch, trying to make her as comfortable as possible.

Frances tried to speak words of comfort to those who came to visit and care for her. She told them, "And oh, how I want you to speak bright, bright words about Jesus, oh do. It's all perfect peace, I am only waiting for Jesus to take me in."[132] She was living the words of her song, "Perfect Peace," which later became known as "Like a River Glorious." Frances had written it while in Leamington, waiting to recover from her prolonged illness.

She spoke little messages of hope for others to deliver to the women at the YWCA where she had ministered so faithfully. Her mind was on encouraging others to follow the Lord. One evening, the doctor visited and left, telling her he most likely would not see her again. Her response was, "Beautiful, too good to be true. Splendid to be so near the gates of heaven. So beautiful to go. Come, Lord Jesus, and take me."[133] At dawn, she slept for a few moments and awakened to say, "He has not failed one word of all His good promises. Tell them to trust in Jesus."[134] Those by her bedside sang along with her, "Jesus, I Will Trust Thee" at her request.

> "Jesus, I will trust Thee,
> Trust Thee with my soul;
> Guilty, lost, and helpless,
> Thou hast made me whole:
> There is none in Heaven
> Or on earth like Thee;
> Thou hast died for sinners,
> Therefore, Lord, for me!"[135]

Frances Ridley Havergal, age 42, entered the presence of her precious Jesus with a song on her lips on June 3, 1879. Frances once explained that "Consecration is not so much a step as a course; not so much an act, as a position to which a course of action inseparably belongs.... We do not want to go on taking a first step over and over again. What we want now, is to be maintained in that position, and to fulfill that course."[136] Frances illustrated with her life how she fulfilled that course of true consecration.

8

Philip Bliss

"Hallelujah! What a Savior"

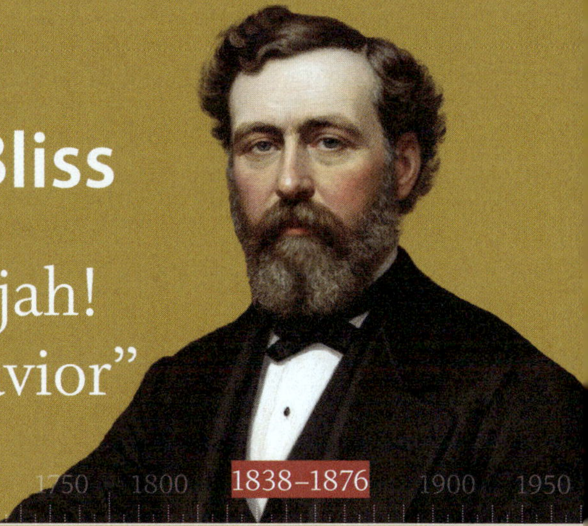

D. 1550 1600 1650 1700 1750 1800 **1838–1876** 1900 1950

"For the Son of God, who came … Ruined sinners to reclaim,"

Hymn: "Hallelujah, What a Savior"

Who Was Philip Bliss?

Philip Paul Bliss was an American composer, hymnwriter, and bass-baritone Gospel singer. He wrote hundreds of well-known hymns, including "Hold the Fort" (1870), "Almost Persuaded" (1871), "Hallelujah, What a Savior!" (1875), "Let the Lower Lights Be Burning," "Jesus Loves Even Me," "Dare to Be a Daniel," "Wonderful Words of Life" (1875), and the melodies for Horatio Spafford's "It Is Well with My Soul" and Frances Havergal's "I Gave My Life for Thee."

The Early Years

Philip Paul Bliss was born in a log cabin on July 9, 1838, in Clearfield County, Pennsylvania. His father and mother were Christians, and both were blessed with musical ability. Philip developed a passion for music from an early age. Singing together was a daily practice in the Bliss family. Philip's father Isaac would lead the family in prayers every day. The family attended a Methodist church regularly. A desire to follow the Lord was ingrained in Philip early.

When Philip was six, his father moved the family to Trumbull City, Ohio. They were only there for three years, then returned to Pennsylvania and settled in Tioga City. During his early years, Philip had little formal teaching. His mother taught him the basics, and his father taught him much doctrine through songs. The Bible was the main influence in his childhood and remained so throughout his life.

Magnificent Music

disheartened: crestfallen

When Philip was ten, he would often go to town, barefooted, to sell vegetables from door to door. This helped add to the family income. One Saturday as he was doing this, he was fascinated by the sweetest sound he had ever heard, coming from a country estate. Without thinking, he climbed the fence and entered the parlor of this elaborate home, unnoticed, to see a young woman playing the piano. Philip had never seen a piano before and stood awestruck as he listened. When she paused in playing, he blurted out, "O lady, please play some more."[138] The lady, quite startled, shouted, "Get out of here with your big bare feet!"[139] Philip quickly left, **disheartened** as he had meant no harm.

Profession of Faith

In 1849, when Philip was 11, he left home to earn money. His mother had tears in her eyes as he headed down the road, but realized it had to be done. He began working at a neighboring farm.

Philip made a public profession of his faith at a revival meeting when he was 12. He told the preacher, "I've always believed in Jesus and asked Him to forgive my sins but now I want to say it out loud."[140] He was baptized and joined the Baptist Church of Cherry Flats, Pennsylvania.

rowdy: noisy, undisciplined

In 1851, he became the assistant cook in a lumber camp for nine dollars a month. Two years later, he was promoted to log cutter. The following year, he began to work in the sawmill. In between jobs, Philip attended school because he had a great desire to learn. He retained his Christian testimony and remained strong spiritually even when working among **rowdy** men. He spent some of his income to get a music education. He also participated in Methodist revival services and camp meetings.

Philip Becomes a Teacher

At 17, Philip went to Bradford City, Pennsylvania, to complete his teaching certification. He was hired a year later by the school board in Hartsville, New York, which was close to his old Pennsylvania home. He taught in a one-room schoolhouse. Whenever possible he attended training seminars to continue his education. During the summer, he worked on farms for income.

In 1857, he met J.G. Towner, who conducted a singing school in Towanda, Pennsylvania. Philip decided to attend. Upon entering the school, Professor Towner told the students to turn to page one and sing "O for a Thousand Tongues." Philip loved Charles Wesley's hymns. He sang with all his might. During the next lesson, Professor Towner said, "Mr. Bliss, you appear to have a vigorous voice, just right for this bass solo. Please stand and begin verse two."[141] Philip silently asked God to help him, then poured his heart into the song. When it ended, he was startled by the loud applause filling the room. By the end of the school term, Bliss and Towner had become good friends.

Professor Towner suggested Philip attend a conference for music teachers in Rome, Pennsylvania, later that year. He told Philip that William Bradbury, a well-known composer of hymns and Sunday School songs, would be there. He encouraged Philip, saying that he was sure Bradbury would be able to help Philip develop his already exceptional voice. Bradbury would later write the music to Bliss's "Jesus Loves Me." Bradbury led a 1,000-member children's choir in New York City. Philip could not have known, but Bradbury would greatly **impact** Philip's future ministry to children through the Sunday School movement. Through Bradbury's influence, Philip decided to become a music teacher.

impact: affect

Still a teen, Philip decided to try his hand at composing music. He sent his first song to **George Root** with a strange note. Not expecting an answer, he wrote, "If you think this song is worth anything, I would appreciate having a flute in exchange for it."[142]

George Root: a famous music instructor and publisher

procured: obtained

Meeting Lucy

Philip was convinced he should stay in Rome and **procured** a teaching job there. He joined the choir in the Presbyterian church. O.F. Young, a school board member, was also the choir director.

Hearing Philip sing, Pastor Darwin Cook commented to Mr. Young, "That young man's voice is worth a thousand dollars a year. Perhaps he does not know it."[143]

O.F. Young and his wife invited Philip to board with them and their five children since he needed a place to stay. The entire Young family enjoyed music. Each evening they gathered around the piano to sing hymns.

Philip soon became attracted to Lucy, the Young's oldest daughter. Her insightful answers in Bible classes at church impressed him. He finally worked up the courage to ask her to marry him, and the couple was married on June 1, 1859. They lived in the Young home for some time while Philip saved up money. He worked as a farm hand for his father-in-law for $13 a month and gave music lessons on winter evenings for $2 an evening.

First Song Published

Philip was concerned that he lacked musical knowledge. He longed to be able to attend a conference at the Normal Academy of Music in Geneseo, New York. The cost was $30 — $30 more than Philip had to spare. Lucy's grandmother overheard him one evening appealing to God in prayer for the money, and she surprised him with the $30 she had been saving. He determined that she would not regret the investment. After the six-week school, he felt prepared to **embark** on a new business of teaching music in earnest. His father-in-law was happy to supply him with a horse named "Old Fanny" and a **melodeon**. For the next three years, he taught music, farmed, and attended classes.

In 1865, Philip had his first song published by **Root & Cady Music Company**. His acceptance was accompanied by a package. As he tore it open, he read, "Our compliments to an excellent musician."[144] In the box was a flute! Philip thought Mr. Root had forgotten him! He was so overwhelmed he had to fight back tears! He hurried to tell Lucy.

embark: launch

melodeon: small organ

Root & Cady Music Company: a successful Chicago-based music publishing company

Root & Cady

Root & Cady offered Philip a salary of $150 per month plus expenses. They assured him that he could bring Lucy when he traveled. In 1864, the couple moved to Chicago which would be their headquarters. Philip's job would be to hold conferences, sing in concerts, and teach Root & Cady's music in churches. Philip's teaching conferences began attracting hundreds of people who wanted to learn under such a gifted musician. He began writing several hymns and Sunday school songs. Many of these were selected for inclusion in the two books, *The Triumph* and *The Prize*, a collection edited by George Root. Root said, "Mr. Bliss was constantly composing, and I soon saw that there was a man who had a 'call' both as a poet and melodist. His songs have been a wonderful power for good."[145] Philip was becoming a popular soloist in concerts. Occasionally, Lucy sang the alto part in duets with Philip. She also worked at Root & Cady's store in downtown Chicago when they were not on the road.

Bliss Meets Moody

One hot summer night in 1869 while taking a walk to buy ice cream, Philip and Lucy ventured into a revival meeting held by the famous D.L. Moody. Before Moody spoke, a song leader led the congregation in several hymns. He was often off-key and got the words confused. Philip cringed but sang loud and clear with his booming bass voice. Philip enjoyed Moody's sermon and was delighted to observe how many people went forward giving their lives to Christ. After the meeting, Moody made a point to find Philip to thank him for rescuing the song service. He explained that his usual song leader was ill. He made Philip promise to lead the singing whenever he was in town. Moody commented to George Root: "Where have you been hiding Bliss for four years? Sending him out of town to sing for everyone else! How is it no one in Chicago has heard him?"[146] "It was hearing the magnificent voice of Mr. Bliss that gave Mr. Moody his idea of engaging a full-time 'gospel singer' to aid him in his revival work."[147]

Major Daniel Whittle, an evangelist who worked with Dwight Moody, said, "What a singer! No meeting can languish when Philip Bliss leads the song service!"[148] Whittle and Bliss became lifelong friends, and Whittle later wrote a biography of the life of Philip Bliss. In 1870, Whittle preached a sermon about a Civil War incident where a group of soldiers were told to hold the fort — help was on the way. Philip went home and wrote the words to the hymn, "Hold the Fort!"

> "Fierce and long the battle rages,
> But our Help is near;
> Onward comes our Great Commander
> Cheer, my comrades, cheer!
> Hold the fort, for I am coming,
> Jesus signals still.
> Wave the answer back to heaven,
> By Thy grace, we will."[149]

Major Whittle recommended Bliss to his pastor Dr. Goodwin for the position of music director at the First Congregational Church in Chicago. Dr. Goodwin was delighted to invite him. Goodwin commented that when a service was growing listless, Philip would "break out with one of his ringing songs that would go through all the hearts like the blast of a bugle and set everything astir."[150] Philip and Lucy spent the next three happy years there, living some of the time with the Whittle family. While there, Philip Paul Bliss Jr. was born in 1872, and George Goodwin Bliss in 1874.

One night Philip, weary from travel, was resting at the Whittle home. He was meditating on Romans 5:5. His heart was overflowing with joy. He took a pencil and paper and began to write, "I am so glad that our Father in heaven, Tells of His love in the Book He has given …."[151] Thus, "Jesus Loves Even Me" was composed.

Philip directed the choir in front of a stained-glass window that showcased a large red cross. He told the congregation, "I am glad we have the cross always before us. Let us forget everything else

when we sing. Let us seek to have the people lose sight of us, of our efforts, our skill, and think only of Him who died thereon, and of the peace, comfort, strength, and joy He gives them that trust Him."[152]

Sunday School Superintendent

Not long after taking the position of Music Director, Philip also took on the responsibility of Sunday School Superintendent. He wrote songs like "Dare To Be a Daniel." In 1873, he wrote and edited a Sunday school hymnal, *The Sunshine*. He became increasingly interested in reaching the hearts of children. He said, "You may have a flower garden without a fountain or a summer day without the sunshine; but do not expect a wide-awake, stirring, effective Sunday school — a school that shall enjoy a healthful popularity, and be in the highest sense successful, without Sunday school singing."[153] He reminded people that Jesus welcomed the children and proposed that the church should do no less.

Moody invited Bliss to travel to England with him to be his music director, but Bliss turned him down. He could not bear the thought of leaving Lucy or his two children for long periods. Instead, Moody took Ira Sankey. Sankey often used compositions Bliss had written and reported that the Britishers loved Bliss' upbeat songs such as "Hold the Fort" and "Jesus Loves Me."

A Sermon in Song

At one of the services conducted by Whittle and Bliss, Philip sang "Almost Persuaded." As he sang, sinners flocked forward for prayer, and many souls were converted. Bliss thought, "To think a song of mine could play a part in their salvation! Thank you, Lord!"[154] He had been inspired to write this song in the early 1870s while listening to a sermon by Reverend Brundage, a friend of his from a little church in the east. Brundage closed his sermon by saying, "He who is almost persuaded is almost saved. But to be almost saved is to be eternally lost."[155]

Both Bliss and Whittle decided that night to join forces as a team and dedicate their lives to full-time evangelism. Whittle later wrote, "Up to the day of his death, I never heard him express a regret that he made his surrender and gave himself to God for His work."[156]

Philip compiled a songbook to use during their campaigns entitled *Gospel Songs*. It proved a tremendous success, and they collected royalties of $30,000. Bliss contributed all **proceeds** to Whittle for the development of their evangelistic ministry. Later, they contributed $60,000 to various charities. When Moody and Sankey returned from England, they combined Sankey's book, *Sacred Songs and Solos*, with Bliss's book and named the new book *Gospel Hymns and Sacred Songs* by Bliss and Sankey.

Bliss and Whittle held over 25 campaigns in Illinois, Wisconsin, Alabama, Pennsylvania, Kentucky, Minnesota, Mississippi, and Georgia. Philip's revival schedule was so full that he had to resign as choir director at the First Congregational Church. He treasured every moment he spent at home with his wife and boys. He and Lucy named their modest home "The Cottage of Content."[157]

proceeds: funds collected from the sale of the book

Singing to Pastors

On Friday, November 24, 1876, Philip sang at a meeting of pastors conducted by D.L. Moody in Chicago. Over 1,000 pastors were present. Here Bliss introduced a new song for which he had written the music: "It Is Well with My Soul." The words were written by his friend Horatio Spafford; the music by Philip Bliss. He also sang "Are Your Windows Open Toward Jerusalem?," a song he had been inspired to write after hearing Horatio Spafford preach. Spafford's sermon was about Daniel, and he was speaking to prisoners in jail in Joliet. "Do not fear to tread the fiery furnace, Nor shrink the lion's den to share; For the God of Daniel will deliver, He will send His angel there."[158]

Next, he conducted a service for 800 prisoners at the Michigan State Prison at Jackson. He tenderly spoke of their homes and children who missed their papas. He told them about his little boy who prays for his papa and his ministry. He appealed to them that there was no way he could give his little boy up to die for others. He said through tears, "Oh, friends, I could not do it, but this is what God did for you. He loved you and gave His son to die for you."[159] Then, still through tears, he sang for them, "Hallelujah! What a Savior."

"Man of Sorrows, what a Name
For the Son of God, who came
Ruined sinners to reclaim,
Hallelujah, What a Savior!
Bearing shame and scoffing rude,
In my place condemned he stood,
Sealed my pardon with His blood.
Hallelujah, what a Savior!
Guilty, vile, and helpless we,
Spotless Lamb of God was He
Full atonement, can it be?
Hallelujah, what a Savior!
Lifted up was He to die,
'It is finished' was His cry,
Now in heaven, exalted high.
Hallelujah, what a Savior!"[160]

Two-thirds of the inmates wept as their expressions softened and their hearts "melted like wax."[161] Many gave their lives in genuine repentance to the Lord that night. It was the last time Philip Bliss would sing.

A Tragic Accident

Philip and Lucy loaded the boys up to head home for Christmas in December 1876. What a joyous Christmas they enjoyed in Rome, Pennsylvania, with Philip's mother and sister! Philip cut down a large evergreen tree the family had fun decorating. There were presents for everyone, and Christmas carols were sung by all. D.L. Moody requested Philip return for a service to be held the Sunday following Christmas. Philip and Lucy decided to leave Philip Paul, age 1, and George, age 4, with Grandma since they did not plan to be gone long.

trestle: short spans supported by closely spaced frames usually carrying a railroad line

extricate: release

On December 29, Philip and Lucy boarded a train, the Pacific Express, headed for Chicago. They encountered a blinding snowstorm along the way. Eleven coaches, being pulled by two engines, were slowly making their way through huge drifts approaching Ashtabula, Ohio. As they passed over a **trestle** bridge that spanned the river, the first engine reached the other side, but all the other cars fell 75 feet down into the icy water. It was later determined that flood waters had weakened the bridge.

Fire broke out five minutes after the train crashed. The wooden cars were soon ablaze. Philip managed to crawl to safety through a window, but discovered that Lucy was pinned under the iron seats. He desperately tried to **extricate** her but was unsuccessful. He bravely made the decision to stay by his wife's side and go to heaven side by side. Out of 160 passengers, only 14 survived.

On December 31, D.L. Moody spoke at a memorial service in Chicago. On January 5, a memorial song service was held to honor Philip Bliss — 8,000 people filled the hall, with 4,000 more waiting outside. The nation mourned. Sunday school children collected $9,500 in pennies to pay for his gravestone and support his orphaned children, Paul and Georgie. D.L. Moody raised $10,000 for the support of the Bliss children, as well as funds for his mother. Philip had sent his trunk ahead to Chicago on another train. In it was the last song Philip Bliss wrote:

> "So, I go on, not knowing;
> I would not if I might
> I'd rather walk in the dark with God;
> Than go alone in the light;
> I'd rather walk by faith with Him
> Than go alone by sight."[162]

Also in his trunk was a manuscript bearing the lyrics of the only well-known Bliss Gospel song for which he did not write a tune: "I Will Sing of My Redeemer." Soon after his death, it was set to music specially written for it by **James McGranahan**. It has become a favorite and was one of the first songs recorded by Thomas Edison. There were many tributes and memorial services held in Philip's memory. D.L. Moody said, "It was in the midst of a terrible storm that he passed away, but the lights that he kindled are burning all along the shore. He had died young, but his hymns are sung round the world."[163]

James McGranahan: a dear friend who would fill Philip's place in the Moody revival services

9

Ira Sankey

Singing the Gospel

1550 1600 1650 1700 1750 1800 **1840–1908** 1950 2000

"But oh, the joy when I shall wake, Within the palace of the King."

Hymn: "Saved by Grace"

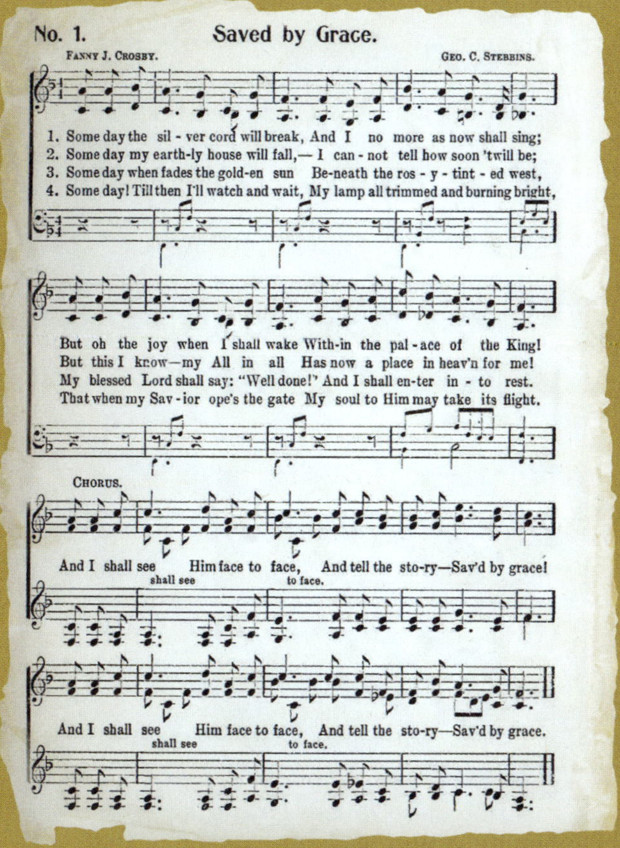

Who Was Ira Sankey?

Ira Sankey was an American Gospel singer and composer. He led the singing for D.L. Moody's evangelistic services in America and Britain in the late 1800s. He composed the music for many beloved hymns that are still sung today. He was one of the first to encourage musical instruments in church services. He had a rich voice that carried well. It was said that Moody "preached the Gospel" and Sankey "sang the Gospel." Some of the more well-known hymns for which he wrote the music are: "Am I a Soldier of the Cross?" "Faith is the Victory," "Send the Gospel Light," "Onward, Christian Soldiers," "A Shelter in the Time of Storm," "The Lily of the Valley," "The Ninety and Nine," and "Thou Didst Leave Thy Throne."

Early Years

Ira David Sankey, son of David and Mary Sankey, was born on August 28, 1840, in the little town of Edinburg on the Mahoning River in western Pennsylvania. His father worked as a banker, then a revenue collector for the federal government, and then a state

senator. Ira, his parents' fifth child, had four brothers and four sisters. In his autobiography, he relates, "As a boy, it was one of my chief joys to meet with the other members of our family around the great log fire in the old homestead, and spend the long winter evenings singing with them the good old hymns of the church … my father would sing a splendid bass, while other members of the family carried the other parts. In this way, I learned to read music."[164]

converted: became a Christian

Ira regularly attended Sunday school, which was held in an old schoolhouse. When he was 16, he was **converted** while attending revival meetings at King's Chapel, a church about three miles from his home.

The Family Moves

In 1857, the family moved to New Castle, Pennsylvania, where his father took a job as bank president. Here, the family joined the Methodist Episcopal Church where Ira became a Sunday school teacher, superintendent of the Sunday school, and choir director. After completing high school, he accepted a job at the bank. When he was 20, he attended a musical convention for choir directors led by the famous composer William Bradbury. When he returned, his father commented, "I'm afraid that boy will never amount to anything; all he does is run about the country with a hymnbook under his arm."[165] His mother was glad he did.

Civil War

In the spring of 1860, President Lincoln called for 75,000 troops to serve 90 days to attempt to prevent the southern states from seceding from the Union. Ira and his brother Charles were among the first in New Castle to volunteer. They became part of Pennsylvania's Twelfth Regiment, Company H. His company was sent to Maryland. "Religious services were held in the camp, and

I often led the singing. I soon found several other young men who could render the same service. In a short time, the people around us also learned there were some singers in the Union camp, and we were frequently invited out by families who had heard of the singing of the 'boys in blue.' The singing of hymns in homes dispelled all feeling of enmity and the soldiers were treated with utmost hospitality and kindness."[166] "At the Cross" was a favorite hymn sung in the homes of citizens.

Maryland had not officially seceded, and there was division among the citizens. In a skirmish in Baltimore, 4 soldiers and 12 civilians were killed. Bridges had been destroyed. Train service between Harrisburg and Baltimore had just reopened. Ira's regiment had the task of guarding to ensure that it remained open. All the men rotated turns on guard duty, keeping a sharp eye out for the enemy. During slow times, Ira was often heard singing. He wrote, "I organized a male choir in the company to which I belonged, and we would frequently be called upon to assist the chaplain in conducting the religious services of the camp."[167]

At the end of his term, Ira did not re-enlist, but went home to assist his father, who had been appointed by President Lincoln as a collector of internal revenue for the 24th Congressional District. Congress had authorized the government to collect income taxes to finance the war. Ira took a job in his father's tax office. It offered a nice salary.

Ira Gets Married

Ira had known Fanny Edwards since his family had first moved to New Castle. She was a member of the church choir he led, and shared his passion for music. She had also attended Bible studies he taught. After returning from the war, he began to take notice of Fanny, and in September 1863, the couple was married. Their son, Harry, was born in 1865. After work each day, Ira and Fanny studied music together. On weekends, they traveled together throughout Ohio and Pennsylvania, where Ira's singing was in great demand. He **pored** over hymnbooks and loved learning new hymns and tunes that he taught to the choir.

In 1867, he helped establish the New Castle branch of the **YMCA**, an organization committed to the spiritual growth of young men. He soon was elected as their president. In 1870, he was appointed a delegate to the International Convention of the Association for the YMCA to be held in Indianapolis. D.L. Moody, the famous evangelist who had organized a large Sunday school ministry in Chicago with 60 teachers and more than 650 students, was one of the speakers at this convention.

pored: read or studied attentively

YMCA: Young Men's Christian Association

Meeting D.L. Moody

During the conference, Ira arrived a bit late. He slipped into the congregation taking a seat next to his friend Reverend Robert McMillan, another delegate from his own county. Robert leaned over and whispered, "Mr. Sankey, the singing here has been abominable; I wish you would start up something when that man stops praying."[168] When he had finished, Ira began singing, "There Is a Fountain Filled with Blood." He was joined by an enthusiastic congregation. At the end of the meeting, he was introduced to Mr. Moody. This is how he described the meeting:

"Moody's first words to me, after my introduction, were, 'Where are you from? Are you married? What is your business?' Upon answering him he abruptly said, 'You will have to give that up — to come to Chicago and help me in my work."[169] Ira told him that he could not leave his business, but Moody persisted, explaining that he had been looking for someone like Ira for the last eight years. Ira promised to pray about it.

The following day, Ira received a note from Moody requesting a meeting with him at a particular street corner at 6 p.m. When Ira arrived, Moody rolled a big box into the street and asked Ira to climb upon it and sing. Ira sang, loud and clear, "Am I a Soldier of the Cross?" A large crowd gathered, and Moody began talking. He ended his 20-minute sermon by asking, "And what does it mean to be His soldier?"[170]

Moody then invited those listening to come to the Opera House to continue the meeting. He asked Ira to lead the men in song as they walked down the street. Ira chose "Shall We Gather at the River?" The Opera House was packed with eager listeners, and many responded to the Gospel message. So, before he headed home, Ira had a glimpse of how his ministry of song **complemented** Moody's ministry of words.

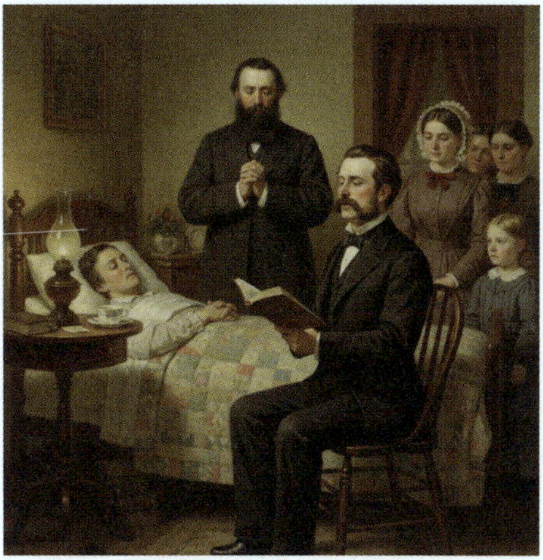

complemented: enhanced

apprehensive: worried, uneasy

Working with Moody

It took Sankey six months to finally consent to spend a week in Chicago with Moody. He asked his wife, his father, and his pastor for counsel, and all agreed it sounded like an opportunity custom-made for him. Once in Chicago, Moody put Ira to work accompanying him on home visits, singing and praying with those who were sick. They held daily prayer meetings at noon and services in the evenings. Moody left the music totally up to Ira. Ira planned the congregational songs, solos, and invitation songs. They ministered to large groups that met in Farwell Hall, which had been the first home of the YMCA.

On a windy Sunday evening in October 1871, near the end of a meeting, bells were heard throughout the city. It had been an unusually hot, dry summer, and several fires had broken out during the fall. Chicago was built largely of wooden structures. People became **apprehensive**. The meeting was dismissed and thousands of listeners flooded out of Farwell Hall to see what was happening. The bells grew louder, and the wind began gusting. Moody and Sankey shook hands and parted ways.

The Chicago Fire

Ira went to collect his belongings and see if he could help others. The city was in chaos as people desperately tried to flee the flames. Entire rows of houses burned. The firefighters were waging a losing battle. Ira finally managed to reach the unburned end of the Fort Wayne and Chicago Railway and found an outbound train for Pennsylvania and home. He later learned that Farwell Hall had burned to the ground, and much of the city lay in ashes. He made it home safely, but it was two months before he heard again from Moody.

Chicago Rebuilds

New buildings were going up quickly. Moody had a temporary structure in which to hold meetings. Moody was engaged in raising funds to not only rebuild his church but also help families in need. He asked Sankey to return to the city. This time, Ira planned to take his family. He went ahead to find suitable lodgings.

Plunging into the work with Moody, he observed that noon prayer meetings were more heavily attended than before the fire. Nightly meetings drew crowds of 1,000 or more. Ira began teaching Sunday school. He started each lesson with a song, and many **opted** to attend his classes. By the fall of 1872, he felt it

opted: chose

was safe to bring Fanny, Harry, and Eddie to the city. Just before they arrived, Moody left for his second evangelistic trip to England. He left Ira in charge, assisted by Major Whittle, a well-known Chicago businessman who later gave up his business to enter upon evangelistic work, and two other faithful men.

Ministering in England

In June 1873, the Moody family and Ira and his wife met in England. They held evangelistic services at the Independent Chapel in London. Hundreds of people soon began responding. Attendance grew and soon more than 20,000 people came to the meetings. They had to start using the **Agriculture Hall** in London to accommodate the crowds. As their fame spread, they were invited by a pastor in Sunderland to hold meetings there.

Upon arrival in the city of Sunderland, they spotted posters containing the following notice: "D.L. Moody of Chicago will 'preach the Gospel,' and Ira D. Sankey of Chicago will 'sing the Gospel' in Bethesda Chapel every afternoon and evening this week."[171] From that time on, the phrase "sing the Gospel" was used to describe Sankey's song ministry. While in London, Mr. R.C. Morgan, editor of *The Christian* newspaper, offered to print up musical pamphlets of the songs used at their meetings. The pamphlet was entitled *"Sacred Songs and Solos sung by Ira D. Sankey at the meetings of Mr. Moody of Chicago."*[172] He printed 500 copies which sold for **sixpence** per copy. A few days later more were ordered.

Agriculture Hall: a large building for holding cattle shows that was often rented for other events

sixpence: about six cents

They eventually printed and distributed over 1,200 pieces. "Little Sankeys," as his pamphlets were called, were reaching new cities. Within a few years, *Sacred Songs and Solos* brought in royalties sufficient to construct the first buildings for a school Moody dreamed of establishing in Northfield, Massachusetts. His plan was to **found** a school with low enough tuition to allow poor girls to receive an education. Ira did not hesitate to **earmark** the money for Moody's project. That dream was realized later in 1879 when Northfield Seminary for Young Ladies was instituted, followed two years later by Mount Hermon School for Boys.

Invitations to speak kept arriving. In Liverpool, Moody and his ministry team met at Victoria Hall which had been erected specifically for their use. It accommodated 10,000 people and was filled 18 times per week. In London, they held services twice each day except for Saturdays in a great hall that seated 14,000.

Ira enjoyed teaching people new songs. He introduced "In the Sweet By and By" and "Christ Arose," among others. By the end of the week, he heard these songs being sung throughout the city. One night, Ira noticed people singing along with him in the service. He broached the idea to Fanny of organizing choirs from among the listeners. The idea was an instant success.

found: establish with provision for the future

earmark: designate

Scotland

In 1873, the team turned its attention to Scotland. They were welcomed warmly. In a quiet room in Scotland, Ira made his first attempt at setting a text to music. It would not be his last. One evening, while scanning a newspaper, Ira saw a poem written by Elizabeth Clephane. The words impressed him as being perfect for a Gospel song. The next day, Moody asked him to sing a song to close a service. Ira prayed, "Father, let me sing so people will hear and understand."[173] He began with an A-flat chord and slowly sang the words of the song:

> "There were ninety and nine that safely lay
> in the shelter of the fold;
> But one was out on the hills away,
> Far off from the gates of gold
> Away on the mountains wild and bare;
> Away from the tender Shepherd's care."[174]

He sang the other two verses and ended with:

> "Rejoice — for the Lord brings back His own."[175]

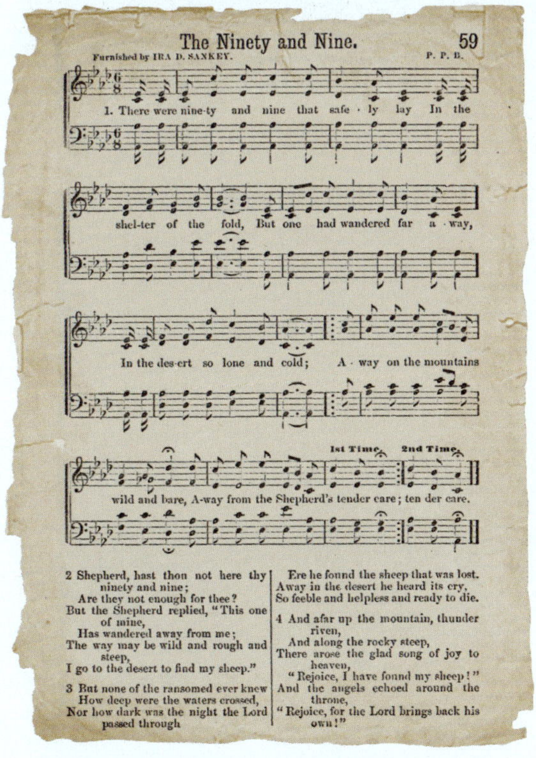

Tears were in many eyes, including Moody's, as many were touched by the words. The song "The Ninety and Nine" soon **circulated** worldwide.

The ministry of Moody and Sankey spread through Scotland and Ireland. Sankey always sang using a small organ for accompaniment. Initially, people didn't

> **circulated:** to become well-known or widespread

approve of playing an instrument in church, but they soon realized that Sankey used the organ to set and keep the tune on key. He strongly felt that the accompaniment should complement the words, not overpower or distract from them. His practice was to request the congregation to join him in prayer, asking God to bless the truth about to be sung. When listeners were moved by the words coming from

his marvelous voice, they all agreed that Sankey indeed "sang the gospel." Attitudes of the congregations changed about the use of musical accompaniment. Moody and his team were flooded with specific testimonies of lives changed by their Gospel message.

Home to America

In August 1875, the Sankeys and Moody headed back to America. For most of 1876, and on and off for the next 20 years, Moody and Sankey traveled the United States, holding meetings, preaching, and singing the Gospel. At one meeting in Brooklyn, New York, the auditorium seating 5,000 was filled, and 15,000 people were turned away for lack of room. The team also traveled several more times to Great Britain.

In 1898, Ira and Fanny traveled to Israel and Egypt, touring and singing. Ira began to tire easily. He began traveling less but started working on compiling a book, *The Story of the Gospel Hymns*. It contained all the letters and testimonies from people who had been blessed by his ministry through the years. He included stories about the impact made in others' lives by many favorite hymns.

One of the most compelling stories he related happened on Christmas Eve 1876. He was traveling on a riverboat heading up the Delaware River. The ship's captain insisted he sing the passengers a song as a conclusion to their festive evening meal. At first, he thought he would sing a Christmas song, but felt strongly impressed that he should instead sing, "Savior, Like a Shepherd Lead Us." When he finished singing, a rough-looking man approached him and asked if he had ever served in the Union Army. Ira replied that he had. The man then asked if he remembered doing **picket** duty on a bright moonlit night in 1862. Sankey replied that he did recall such a night. "The man explained that he had served in the Confederate army and one night he'd had Sankey in his gun sights … and then Sankey had begun to sing that same song."[176]

The stranger said the song brought back memories of his God-fearing mother who had sung it to him many times when he was a boy. He told Sankey that when the song was over, his arm dropped limp at his side, and he could not bring himself to shoot. Through his tears, he confessed that ever since then, he had lived a broken life. He begged Sankey to help him find rest in that Savior he had sung about. Ira threw his arms around the **penitent** man who had once been his enemy. That Christmas Eve, Sankey led the man to faith in Jesus Christ.

picket: guard

penitent: sorrowful

"It seemed that the Lord was shepherding Sankey safely through the war, even in the presence of his enemies."[177] Sankey never tired of hearing about the life-changing impact his beloved songs had on so many people. The book was completed in 1906.

As Sankey grew older, he struggled with congestive glaucoma that caused his eyesight to eventually fail. He drew great encouragement from his dear friend Fanny Crosby, the blind songwriter. He had set many of her hymns to music, such as "Saved by Grace." He especially liked the verse:

> "Some day, the silver cord will break,
> And I no more as now shall sing;
> But oh, the joy when I shall wake
> Within the palace of the King.
> And I shall see Him face to face
> And tell the story — Saved by Grace."[178]

On August 13, 1908, Ira Sankey went home to his Savior. "The New York Times reported that he was faintly singing Crosby's song as he died, 'But oh, the joy when I shall wake within the palace of the King.' "[179]

10

Ten Famous Hymns and Their Writers

Shorter Biographies of Ten Hymnwriters

This chapter will teach us about ten hymnwriters who composed some of our favorite hymns. Although we do not have as much biographical information about their lives as others in this book, we have enough to encourage us by what inspired them to write hymns that have blessed Christians through the ages.

Williams Pantycelyn

"Guide Me, O Thou Great Jehovah"

1717–1791

Williams Pantycelyn was born in Llandovery, Wales, in 1717, the son of a farmer. In 1740, he was studying to become a doctor. During this time, he was also a deacon of the **Anglican** Church. Hearing the sweet sound of bells from a steeple one day, he felt drawn to go into the church. The service was uninspiring, but when he left, he noticed people standing around and watched as a tall man climbed to the top of a gravestone to speak. He listened intently as a preacher named Howell Harris proclaimed the need for every human being to have his own personal relationship with Jesus Christ. The preacher was involved with a movement led by the Wesleys of England. Williams also met George Whitefield, an itinerate preacher.

Williams left the Anglican Church to join the Methodists. He gave up his desire to pursue medicine and instead devoted his life to being a traveling evangelist. Over the next 43 years, he rode 100,000 miles on horseback, preaching and singing. He became known as "the sweet singer of Wales."[180] He was married in 1748 and his wife, a gifted singer, often accompanied him on his travels.

Anglican: official church of England

Williams wrote over 800 hymns during his lifetime, and is best known for "Guide Me,

O Thou Great Jehovah." This beloved hymn has been translated into 75 different languages. Because the Welsh people were known to be lovers of music, he often used printed copies of his hymns to teach them to read. Welsh miners frequently sang his hymns on their way to work. He was recognized as one of the leaders of the Methodist revival in Wales.

rugby: English football

Williams published his first hymnbook in 1744. Wherever he went, he established local Methodist fellowships so that his converts could continue to meet and worship together after he left. He died on January 11, 1791. He was beloved in Wales. Every year at their **rugby** games, the Welsh people sing "Bread of Heaven," the name the Welsh people gave to "Guide Me, O Thou Great Jehovah" in tribute to Williams Pantycelyn.

Edward Perronet

"All Hail the Power of Jesus' Name"

1726–1792

Edward Perronet was born in 1726. His family, a line of distinguished French Huguenots, had to flee first to Switzerland and then England to avoid religious persecution. Edward was ordained as an Anglican minister but left to join the evangelistic movement begun by John and Charles Wesley. He personally faced opposition when he did this. John Wesley recorded that on one occasion, when they encountered a violent mob, Edward was attacked. “They immediately closed in, threw him down, and rolled him in the **mire**; so that when he scrambled from them and got into the house again, no one could scarcely tell what or who he was.”[181]

mire: swampy mud

At one evening service, John Wesley announced that Edward was the main speaker, much to Edward’s surprise. Edward calmly told the crowd that he would give the greatest sermon ever preached. Then, he opened his Bible and read the Sermon on the Mount from Matthew chapters five through seven.

Edward published many poems and hymns during his lifetime. In 1779, he penned “All Hail the Power of Jesus’ Name,” the hymn that has been called by some “The National Anthem of Christendom.” It was adapted slightly by Oliver Holden in 1792, the year of Edward’s death, and set to the tune of “Coronation.”

E.P. Scott, a missionary to India, tells of one gripping instance in which this hymn was used by God to save lives and bring salvation: “Journeying to a dangerous territory, he suddenly found himself surrounded by spear-wielding tribesmen. Certain he was about to be killed, he took a violin from his baggage and began playing ‘All Hail the Power of Jesus’ Name’! When he dared to look up again, the spears had been lowered, and some tribesmen were crying. Scott stayed for years, sharing the Good News with this ‘kindred,’ this ‘tribe.’”[182]

Edward Perronet died on January 2, 1792, giving glory to God and commending his spirit to his precious Savior.

Robert Robinson

"Come, Thou Fount of Every Blessing"

1735–1790

Robert Robinson was born on September 27, 1735, in Swaffham, England. His father Michael Robinson died when Robert was 14 years old. For financial reasons, Robert had to go to work as a barber's apprentice. When he was 17, he and some rowdy friends went to hear George Whitefield preach in London. The boys intended to disrupt the meeting. Whitefield was preaching that day from Matthew 3 on repentance. Robinson was deeply moved and spent the next two years agonizing about his decision; he finally was converted on December 10, 1755. He wrote on the flyleaf of his Bible, "After tasting the pain of renewal for two years and seven months, I found full absolution and grace through the precious blood of Jesus Christ."[183]

Robert remained in London for a few years, growing in his faith and listening to George Whitefield, John Wesley, and other preachers. Here he trained for the ministry and wrote poetry. He began serving at a Calvinistic Methodist Chapel in 1758. The next year, he joined an independent church and later a Baptist church. During this time, he wrote, "Come, Thou Fount of Every Blessing."

An interesting fact about this song is the word "Ebenezer." This name comes from 1 Samuel 7:12, in which the prophet Samuel raised a stone monument, declaring, "Hitherto hath the Lord helped us (KJV)." He named this stone, "Ebenezer," meaning "Stone of Help."

In this chapter, the Israelites had just recommitted themselves to God; now, they were under attack by the Philistines. Things looked desperate, but Samuel cried out to God for help. God answered powerfully! He sent a massive thunderstorm that panicked the Philistines and enabled the Israelites to win a huge victory. The "Ebenezer Stone" was set up to mark the spot as a perpetual reminder that God will always rescue His people from danger.

Robinson married Ellen Payne in 1759, and the couple was blessed with 12 children. He owned an 80-acre farm where he grew wheat and barley, and raised and sold sheep and cattle. The venture was successful, and in 1782 he purchased more farmland. On June 9, 1790, Robert died peacefully in his sleep at age 75.

Augustus Toplady

"Rock of Ages"

1740–1778

Augustus Toplady was born in Farnham, England, in 1740. He never saw his father, a major in the British army who died at the siege of Carthagena, a war between Spain and Great Britain. His mother was a strong Christian woman he greatly respected. Augustus went to Westminster School in London from 1750 to 1755, when he and his mother moved to Ireland. He attended Trinity College in Dublin and graduated in 1760.

When Augustus was 16, he went to a religious meeting held in a barn in the small village of Codymain. The preacher was James Morris, a follower of John Wesley. Augustus gave his life to the Lord that day. In 1759, he published his first book entitled *Poems on Sacred Subjects*. In 1762, he was ordained as a deacon.

While walking in a rocky glen one day, Augustus was caught in a severe thunderstorm. He spotted a large limestone rock with an opening right down its center. He raced to it, and it shielded him from the torrential downpour. The thought occurred to him that Christ was like a sheltering rock, and from this experience, he was inspired to write "Rock of Ages." This hymn has been a comfort to many Christians encountering the storms of life throughout the years.

When Confederate General J.E.B. Stuart was mortally wounded at Yellow Tavern, Virginia, he asked the minister to sing "Rock of Ages" to him as he lay dying. When Toplady lay dying in 1778, he exclaimed, "I enjoy heaven already in my soul. My prayers are all converted into praises."[184] He was 38 years old when he died.

Reginald Heber

"Holy, Holy, Holy"

1783–1826

Reginald Heber was born in Malpas, Cheshire, England, on April 21, 1783. He was educated at home by his father until he was seven years old, then attended the local school for 10 years. Reginald was extremely generous — his mother had to sew his money into his pockets to prevent him from giving it all away to help others. He also loved entertaining people with well-told stories.

Heber went to school at Oxford University and was ordained at age 26. Later he became the **Vicar** of Hodnet in England. He saw the importance of good congregational singing. Frequently he wrote hymns to complement his sermons. At Hodnet, Reginald wrote "Holy, Holy, Holy," composed especially for Trinity Sunday, the first Sunday after Pentecost. Alfred Lord Tennyson, an English poet who was the Poet Laureate during much of Queen Victoria's reign, called it the most famous hymn of all time.

During his time at Hodnet, Heber wrote 57 hymns. He also spent much time visiting the sick, even at a risk to his own health. He generously gave to the needs of others and assisted in promoting reconciliation and unity in numerous disagreements.

After being in Hodnet for 16 years, Reginald was asked to become the bishop in Calcutta, India,

Vicar: bishop

and sailed there in 1823. It was his responsibility to oversee India, Ceylon, and Australia, to visit churches throughout the regions, confirm new believers, and train others for the ministry. He had been in India for only three years when he died suddenly, leaving a wife and two baby girls. He was 43 years old. The following year, 57 of his hymns were published in a book entitled *Hymns Written and Adapted to the Weekly Service of the Year*.

Edward Mote

"My Hope is Built on Nothing Less"

1797–1874

Edward Mote was born in London on January 21, 1797. His parents ran a **pub**. Because his parents were so busy, Edward was left to amuse himself on the streets. He once said that as a boy he was so ignorant, he did not even know there was a God.

Edward was apprenticed to be a cabinet maker when he was 18. His master brought him to Tottenham Court Road Chapel. There, under the passionate preaching of John Hyatt, he gave his life to Jesus Christ. Edward continued learning the cabinet-building trade and eventually opened his own business. His heart was filled with a deep desire to express his love for Christ through music.

pub: a public house that served drinks and food

One morning in 1834 while walking to his workshop, poetic phrases suddenly began to form in his head: "On Christ the solid Rock, I stand; All other ground is sinking sand."[185] During the day, four **stanzas** materialized. The next Sunday while visiting a friend whose wife was extremely ill, Edward offered to sing the song to her. She took great comfort in it and asked for a copy of the words.

stanzas: divisions of a poem

He wondered if the hymn meant so much to this woman, would others feel the same way about it? He had 1,000 copies printed to share. In 1836, Mote's hymn, now titled "The Solid Rock," was published in *Hymns of Praise, A New Selection of Gospel Hymns*. In 1863, William Bradbury set the hymn to the tune we now sing, and it skyrocketed in popularity.

At 55, Edward Mote became a Baptist preacher at the Strict Street Baptist Church in Horsham, where he faithfully served for 21 years. He wrote more than 150 hymns in his lifetime. His congregation offered to give him the deed to the church property as a token of their gratitude. Mote, however, humbly refused, saying, "I do not want the chapel. I only want the pulpit, and when I cease to preach Christ, then turn me out of that."[186] Edward died at age 77, certain he was going to see his Savior.

Robert Lowry

"Christ Arose,"
"Shall We Gather at the River?"

1826–1899

Robert Lowry was born on March 12, 1826, in Philadelphia, Pennsylvania. He had a deep passion and aptitude for music even as a small child. He loved playing any musical instrument he could get his hands on. When he was 17, Robert became a member of the First Baptist Church of Philadelphia where he joined the choir and began teaching Sunday school. At 22, he entered the University of Lewisburg, Pennsylvania, to prepare for the ministry. He became a pastor when he graduated.

Robert served as pastor in West Chester, Pennsylvania, from 1854 to 1858, in New York City from 1859 to 1861, in Brooklyn, New York, from 1861 to 1858, and in Lewisburg, Pennsylvania, from 1869 to 1875. Then he pastored Park Avenue Church in Plainfield, New Jersey. He had successful ministries in each location. Robert had a pleasant disposition and a good sense of humor. "Very few men had greater ability in painting pictures from their imagination. He could thrill an audience with his vivid descriptions, inspiring others with the same thoughts that inspired him."[187]

Lowry authored many hymns which have been translated into numerous languages. He wrote several hymnbooks for children as well. When asked to describe his method for composing hymns, he answered, "I have no method. Sometimes the music comes, and the words follow, fitted insensibly to the melody. I watch my moods, and when anything good strikes me, whether words or music, and no matter where I am, at home or on the street, I jot it down. Often the margin of a newspaper or the back of an envelope serves as a notebook. My brain is a sort of spinning machine, I think, for there is music running through it all the time. I do not pick out my music on the keys of an instrument. The tunes of nearly all the hymns I have written have been completed on paper before I tried them on the organ. Frequently the words of the hymn and the music have been written at the same time."[188]

Some of Robert Lowry's best-known hymns are: "Shall We Gather at the River?" "I Need Thee Every Hour," "All the Way My Savior Leads Me," "We're Marching to Zion," and "Christ Arose." After a meeting of Sunday school workers in London, the chairman announced that the author of "Shall We Gather at the River?" was in attendance. Lowry was asked to come forward to sing the song. Men applauded and women waved handkerchiefs as he walked forward. Afterward, he commented, "It was a tribute to the hymn; but I felt, when it was over, that, after all, I had perhaps done some little good in the world, and I felt more than ever content to die when God called."[189] On Children's Day in Brooklyn in 1865, this song was sung by more than 40,000 voices.

Dr. Lowry died at his home in Plainfield, New Jersey, on November 25, 1899. His sermons in song still live today in hymnbooks and hearts all over the world.

Annie Hawks

"I Need Thee Every Hour"

1835–1918

Annie S. Hawks was born in Hoosick, New York, on May 28, 1836. She attended both public school and Troy Seminary, although she never graduated from either school. She had a passion for reading and loved to learn. When she was 14 years old, she began submitting poems to the newspaper in Troy, New York.

Annie married when she was 24, and the couple moved to Brooklyn, New York. Eventually, they had three children. In Brooklyn, they joined the church pastored by Robert Lowry, who was a Hymnwriter and a theologian. When he became aware of Annie's gift for writing, Dr. Lowry encouraged her to compose hymns for which he could then supply the music. One day in 1872, Annie handed him a poem entitled "I Need Thee Every Hour." Although Annie wrote about 400 hymns in her lifetime, this one has become a universal favorite. Dwight L. Moody and Ira Sankey used it often in their evangelistic meetings, which helped spread its fame.

Here is Annie's account of what inspired her to write this amazing hymn. "I remember well the morning many years ago when in the midst of the daily cares of my home, I was so filled with a sense of the nearness to my Master, that wondering how one could live without Him either in joy or pain, these words 'I need Thee every hour' flashed into my mind. Seating myself by the open window in the balmy air of the bright June day, I caught up my pencil and the words were soon committed to paper, almost as they are being sung now."[190]

Annie later explained that the words had come to her during a peaceful, joyful time of her life. Sixteen years later when facing a personal sorrow, the death of her husband, she experienced the comforting power of the words she had written years before. She wrote, "I did not understand at first why this hymn had touched the great throbbing heart of humanity. It was not until years after, when the shadow fell over my way, the shadow of a great loss, that I understood something of the comforting power in the words which I had been permitted to give out to others in my hour of sweet serenity and peace."[191] After the death of her husband in 1888, Annie moved to Bennington, Vermont, to live with her daughter and son-in-law. There she died on January 3, 1918.

Lidie Edmunds

"My Faith Has Found a Resting Place"

1851–1920

Eliza Jane Edmunds Hewitt was born on June 28, 1851, in Philadelphia, Pennsylvania, the daughter of a sea captain, James Stratton Hewitt. Her mother was Zeruiah Stites Edmunds. Eliza attended the Girls Normal School in Philadelphia and graduated as the **valedictorian** in her class. She then worked as a schoolteacher at the Northern Home for Friendless Children in Philadelphia.

Eliza had a cheerful, vibrant personality. One day in 1887, a student who was upset at her for being corrected for wrong behavior struck her on the back with a heavy slate. The injury caused a serious spinal problem. Eliza was confined to a heavy cast for six months. She eventually partially recovered but suffered as an invalid for a large part of her life.

Though bedridden, Eliza refused to let bitterness rule her life. She began to study English literature and spent her time writing poems for children. Eliza was probably encouraged to write by her cousin Edgar Stites, who was a hymnwriter. She was also a close friend of Fanny Crosby, the blind author of numerous hymns. Eliza developed Sunday school materials for children and wrote regularly for children's magazines.

Some of Eliza's poems were given to William Kirkpatrick, a famous composer, who liked what he saw and composed music for many of them. She used the **pseudonym** Lidie H. Edmunds for some of her works, including one of her most famous hymns, "My Faith Has Found a Resting Place."

valedictorian: the highest academic achiever of the class

pseudonym: a fictitious name, especially one used by an author

Kirkpatrick found an old Norwegian tune for this hymn, known as "The Hardy Norseman's House of Yore," which he adapted to fit the words. It was published in 1890 in a collection of hymns. It was about 50 years before it grew in popularity; it is now included in most hymnbooks. Eliza also wrote "More About Jesus," "When We All Get to Heaven," and "Will There Be Any Stars?"

Eliza was a member of the Calvin Presbyterian Church in Philadelphia. When she was physically able, she began working in the Sunday school department. She later became Sunday School Superintendent at the Northern Home for Friendless Children as well as the Calvin Presbyterian Church. Eliza died on April 24, 1920, and was buried at the Woodlands Cemetery in Philadelphia.

"My Faith Has Found a Resting Place" reminds us, "As we come before God, we can 'rest our case,' knowing that Jesus has gone to the cross in our place. No other argument is necessary, no other plea. The sacrifice of Jesus is enough."[192]

Thomas Obadiah Chisholm

"Great is Thy Faithfulness"

1866–1960

Thomas Obadiah Chisholm was born in a log cabin in Kentucky in 1866. He lacked formal schooling but was an **avid** learner. He became a schoolteacher at the age of 16. At 21, he took a job as associate editor of his town's newspaper, *The Franklin Advocate*. More importantly, when he was 21, he became a Christian through the ministry of Henry Clay Morrison, the founder of Asbury College and Seminary in Wilmore, Kentucky. From that time on, he focused

avid: enthusiastic

his energies on spreading the Gospel. Thomas was ordained as a Methodist minister and became the pastor of a church in Scottsville, Kentucky, his hometown.

In 1903, Thomas married Catherine Vanderveer, and the happy couple had two little girls. In 1909, he began to experience some health problems which forced him to give up his pastorate. His medical bills grew. Chisholm's life took an unexpected turn, but he refused to become bitter. Instead, he looked for God's blessings in his life. He no longer had a pastorate, but now he had more time to focus on writing hymns.

In his lifetime, he wrote 12,000 poems, 800 of which were published as hymns. He had health struggles, but he also had a devoted wife and two beautiful daughters to love. He directed his thoughts constantly toward God's faithfulness. He often contemplated this verse from Lamentations 3:22–23: "It is of the Lord's mercies that we are not consumed, because his compassions fail not. They are new every morning: great is thy faithfulness (KJV)."

In 1929, he wrote his most famous hymn, "Great Is Thy Faithfulness." He sent the poem to Reverend William Runyan, a musician at the Moody Bible Institute and editor of Hope Publishing Company in Chicago. Runyan had many submissions to consider, but when he saw these words, he was greatly moved. Runyan prayed that his tune might convey the message of the words in a worthy manner. He concluded years later that God had answered his prayer. The song was mightily used by God. It was sung at Moody Bible Institute and was considered the college's favorite hymn. In the 1950s, Billy Graham began using the song at his crusade meetings. What was once a simple hymn gained worldwide acclaim and was sung by millions.

Chisholm lived for many years in Vineland, New Jersey, working as a life insurance agent to support himself and his family. He was able to retire in 1953 and spent his remaining years in a Methodist retirement community in Ocean Grove, New Jersey. Shortly before he died in 1960, Chisholm wrote, "My income has never been large at any time due to impaired health in the earlier years which had followed me on until now. But I must not fail to record here the unfailing faithfulness of a covenant-keeping God and that He has given me many wonderful displays of His providing care which have filled me with astonishing gratefulness."[193]

Timeline

1674 – 1712

1674	Isaac Watts is born on July 17 in Southampton, England
1690	Isaac Watts writes his first hymn, begins attending Newington Academy
1694	Isaac Watts begins his study and writing at home for 2½ years
1696	Isaac Watts becomes tutor to the children of Sir John Hartropp in London
1702	Watts becomes the pastor of Mark Lane Chapel.
1703	John Wesley is born
1706	Isaac Watts publishes his first collection of poetry
1707	Isaac Watts publishes *Hymns and Spiritual Songs*
1707	Charles Wesley is born
1712	Cotton Mather publishes hymns by Isaac Watts in the American colonies

1715 – 1730

1715	Isaac Watts publishes *Divine Songs for Children*
1716	Charles Wesley attends Westminster School
1717	Williams Pantycelyn is born
1719	Isaac Watts publishes *The Psalms of David Imitated in the Languages of the New Testament*
1726	Charles Wesley enrolls at Christ Church, Oxford
1726	Sally Gwynne is born
1726	Edward Perronet is born
1729	Benjamin Franklin publishes Isaac Watt's *Psalms of David*
1729	Charles Wesley keeps a diary
1729	The "Holy Club" is formed
1730	Charles Wesley becomes a tutor at Oxford

1731 – 1738

1731	William Cowper is born on February 15
1732	The "Holy Club" called the Methodists, George Whitefield joins Holy Club
1732	The colony of Georgia is established in America
1735	Samuel Wesley dies
1735	Charles Wesley is ordained as a deacon
1735	Charles Wesley is appointed as Secretary of Indian Affairs in Georgia
1735	Robert Robinson is born
1736	Charles and John Wesley begin ministry in Georgia
1736	Charles Wesley leaves Georgia for England
1737	William Cowper's father sends him to boarding school
1738	Charles Wesley and brother John are converted
1738	George Whitefield begins preaching in the American colonies and uses Watts' hymns

1739 – 1749

1739	Charles Wesley first preaches in the open air
1739	The Wesleys publish *Hymns and Sacred Poems*
1740	Williams Pantycelyn is converted and joins the Wesleys
1740	William Cowper is enrolled in Westminster School
1740	Augustus Toplady is born
1741	William Cowper is enrolled in Westminster School
1742	Jonathan Edwards uses Watt's hymns in his congregation
1742	Susanna Wesley dies, Methodism spreads through England
1744	Williams Pantycelyn's first hymnbook published
1747	Charles and John Wesley begin ministry in Ireland
1748	Isaac Watts dies
1748	John Newton is saved
1748	Williams Pantycelyn is married
1749	Charles Wesley marries Sally Gwynne

1749 – 1767

1749	Charles Wesley publishes his two-volume *Hymns and Sacred Poems*
1749–1756	William Cowper studies law
1755	Robert Robinson is saved
1756	George Whitefield publishes a hymnal
1757	Charles Wesley's first son is born
1758	Robert Robinson writes "Come Thou Fount"
1760	Augustus Toplady graduates from Trinity College in Dublin
1762	Charles Wesley publishes *Short Hymns on Selected Passages of Scripture*–2 Volumes with 2,030 hymns
1763	William Cowper goes to live with Dr. Cotton as a patient
1764	William Cowper is saved
1765	William Cowper moves to Huntingdon, Cambridge, rents from Unwin family
1767	William Cowper meets John Newton

1770 – 1815		
	1770	George Whitefield dies in America
	1770	John Cowper gets saved and dies
	1772–1773	William Cowper writes 68 hymns
	1776	Augustus Toplady writes "Rock of Ages"
	1778	Augustus Toplady dies
	1779	*The Olney Hymnal* is published
	1779	Edward Perronet writes "All Hail the Power"
	1783	Reginald Heber is born
	1790	Robert Robinson dies
	1791	William Pantycelyn dies
	1792	Edward Perronet dies
	1797	Edward Mote is born
	1788	Charles Wesley dies in London
	1799	Wiliam Cowper writes his last poem
	1800	William Cowper dies April 25
	1815	Edward Mote is saved

1820 – 1836		
	1820	Fanny Crosby is born and becomes blind
	1820–1834	Crosby family lived in several sections of New York and Connecticut
	1822	Sally Wesley dies in London
	1823	Reginald Heber goes to Calcutta
	1826	Reginald Heber dies
	1826	Robert Lowry is born
	1828	Horatio Spafford born on October 20
	1829	Invention of Braille printing
	1834	Edward Mote writes "On the Solid Rock"
	1835	Fanny Crosby enters New York Institution for the Blind as a student and then becomes a teacher there until 1858
	1835	Annie Hawks is born
	1836	Frances Havergal is born in Worcestershire, UK

1836 – 1849

1836–1842	Havergals live in Astley where Frances' father is rector
1838	Philip Bliss is born on July 9
1840	Ira Sankey is born on August 28
1841	Fanny Crosby's first published poem
1844	Fanny Crosby's first published book
1844	Bliss family moves to Ohio
1845–1860	Havergals live in St. Nichols rectory in Worcester
1847	Bliss family moves back to Pennsylvania
1848	Frances Havergal's mother dies on July 5
1848	Philip Bliss hears a piano for the first time
1849	Philip Bliss has to go to work at 11 years old
1849	Cholera epidemic in New York City

1850 – 1856

1850	Philip Bliss is saved
1851	Philip Bliss becomes assistant cook in lumber yard
1850–1851	Frances Havergal attends Belmont School for Girls in London
1852–1853	Frances Havergal goes to Germany with her father and writes "I Gave My Life for Thee"
1851–1857	Fanny Crosby and George Root write at least 60 songs
1851	Frances Havergal's father marries Caroline Cooke
1851	Lidie Edmunds is born
1853	Fanny Crosby's second book published
1854–1875	Robert Lowry serves as pastor
1856	Philip Bliss becomes a teacher
1856	Frances Havergal goes to Ireland to minister in song
1856	Ira Sankey is saved
1856	Horatio Spafford moves to Chicago to open law practice

1857 – 1865		
	1857	Sankey family moves to New Castle, Pennsylvania
	1857	Philip Bliss meets J.G. Towner and William Bradbury
	1858	Fanny Crosby marries Alexander Van Alstyne
	1859	Fanny Crosby's only child is born and dies
	1859	Philip Bliss marries Lucy Young
	1859	Frances Havergal's first hymn, "I Gave My Life for Thee," is published
	1860	Ira Sankey meets Wiliam Bradbury at music convention
	1860	Ira Sankey joins the Union Army and organizes a male choir
	1861–1867	Frances Havergal is governess to her nieces in Oakhampton
	1861	Horatio Spafford marries Anna Larssen
	1863	Ira Sankey marries Fanny Edwards
	1865	Baby Harry is born to Ira and Fanny Sankey

1865 – 1870

1865	Philip Bliss's first song is published
1865	Bliss family moves to Chicago
1866	Thomas Chisholm is born
1867	Frances Havergal's first trip to Switzerland (also went in 1871, 1873, 1874, and 1876)
1867	Ira Sankey helps establish New Castle branch of YMCA
1867–1870	Frances Havergal stays with her family in Leamington; joins the YWCA
1864–1915	Fanny Crosby's 50-year career of writing hymns and gospel songs
1869	Philip Bliss meets D.L. Moody
1869	Frances Havergal's first book published: *The Ministry of Song*
1870	Frances Havergal's father dies, April 19
1870	Ira Sankey meets D.L. Moody
1870	Philip Bliss writes "Hold the Fort"
1870	Philip Bliss inspired to write "Almost Persuaded"

1870 – 1873		
	1870s	Invention of the telephone, microphone, phonograph, and incandescent lights
	1870	Frances Havergal's *Sacred Songs for Little Singers* is published
	1870	Horatio Spafford commits to pay part of Moody's salary
	1871	Frances Havergal's *Psalmody* published
	1871	The Chicago Fire in October
	1872	Sankey family relocates in Chicago
	1872	Annie Hawks writes "I Need Thee Every Hour"
	1872	Philip Bliss Jr is born
	1873	Philip Bliss writes and edits *The Sunshine*
	1873	Horatio Spafford's four daughters die at sea in November
	1873	Moody and Sankeys go to conduct meetings in England
	1873	Moody and Sankeys minister in Scotland and Ireland

1874 – 1879

1874	George Bliss is born
1874	Edward Mote dies
1874	Frances Havergal's best known hymn, "Take My Life and Let It Be," is published
1875	Moody and Sankeys return to America
1876	Ira Sankey meets the man who almost killed him during the Civil War; the man gets converted
1876	In November Philip Bliss writes music for and sings "It Is Well with My Soul" for first time
1876	Horatio Spafford, Jr. is born
1876	Philip Bliss and wife Lucy die in train wreck December 29
1878	Frances Havergal's step-mother dies
1878	Frances Havergal goes to stay with sister Maria in Wales
1878	Bertha Spafford is born
1879	Frances Havergal dies

1880 – 1908		
	1880s	Invention of fountain pen, steam turbine, electric trolley car, motorcycle
	1881	Grace Spafford is born
	1881	Spaffords move to Israel
	1887	Lidie Edmunds is injured
	1887	Thomas Chisholm is saved
	1888	Horatio Spafford dies
	1890s	Invention of rayon, zippers, submarine, photography
	1890	"My Faith Has Found a Resting Place" is published
	1899	Robert Lowry dies
	1900s	Invention of the airplane, helicopter, vacuum cleaner
	1902	Fanny Crosby's husband dies
	1903	Thomas Chisholm marries
	1906	*The Story of Gospel Hymns* is completed by Ira Sankey
	1908	Ira Sankey dies on August 13

1915 – 1960		
	1915	Fanny Crosby dies on February 12 just a few days short of her 95th birthday
	1918	Annie Hawks dies
	1920	Lidie Edmunds dies
	1923	Anna Spafford dies
	1929	Thomas Chisholm writes "'Great Is Thy Faithfulness"
	1960	Thomas Chisholm dies

Glossary

abducted: kidnapped, captured

acrid: a strong, unpleasant, irritating smell

acrostic: a poem in which the first letters in each line form a word

affluent: wealthy

Agriculture Hall: a large building for holding cattle shows that was often rented for other events

allocate: give

Anglican Church: the established church in England

anonymously: without identifying the source

apprehensive: worried, uneasy

asylum: an institution offering shelter and support to people who are mentally ill

atheist: a person who does not believe in the existence of God

avid: enthusiastic

Bar Association: an organization of attorneys that certifies a law school graduate as a lawyer

battledore: a game played with a shuttlecock and rackets, a forerunner of badminton

benevolent: giving money to those in need

benumbed: overcome

blasphemies: shows of contempt for God

cajoling: coaxing with gentle persuasion or false promises

circulated: to become well-known or widespread

clothier: a maker of woolen cloth

colleagues: associates

Collegium Insanorum: College of the Insane

commuter train: passenger rail service that primarily operates within a metropolitan area

complimented: enhanced

consecrated: dedicated

consigned: sent

converted: became a Christian

cottage meetings: meetings in homes

deteriorated: grew worse

disheartened: crestfallen

disheartening: losing hope, spirit, or morale

Dissenting: Protestants who separated from the Church of England

dissipate: gradually vanish

distortions: altering something true

doted on: showed great fondness or affection

embark: launch

enamored: to have strong feelings of admiration and love

encore: repeated performance

enhance: improve, make memorable

entrepreneur: one who organizes and operates a business

evacuation plans: preparations to flee

evangelistic: seeking to convert others to Christianity

exorbitant: excessive, overpriced

expelled: sent away

exuberant: joyfully enthusiastic

Fellow: highly respected teacher

filial: due from a son

flourished: thrived

foundry: a factory that produces metal castings by melting, pouring, and solidifying metals into molds

George Root: a famous music instructor and publisher

Great Awakening: a series of religious revivals

Guinea ship: a boat owned by the Guinea Company, which evolved into England's first slave-trading company

hinder: obstruct

House of Lords: the higher chamber of Parliament

hues: colors or shades

Huguenot: French protestant

impact: affect

impeccable: flawless

impetus: driving force

impress: force

invalid: disabled, prevented from living a normal life

irons: shackles, chains

James McGranahan: a dear friend who would fill Philip's place in the Moody revival services

lashed: tied so the storm would not wash him overboard

looters: raiding thieves

lord mayor: a title of a mayor of a major city with special recognition by the king

melodeon: small organ

menial: lowly

meter: a basic repeated pattern of rhythm or music

midshipman: an officer of the lowest rank

mire: swampy mud

Moravian believers: Moravian Church beliefs are solidly grounded in the Bible, under the teachings of Czech reformer John Huss

mortgage: a loan

mutiny: rebellion against authority

native: normally grow

Nonconformist: one who did not conform to certain practices of the established church and was therefore restricted from many areas of public life

opted: chose, decided

ordination: officially setting apart for ministry

overseer: an agent employed by slaveholders to supervise the daily affairs on a plantation

packet boats: designed mainly for domestic mail and freight transport

palatial: splendid

penitent: sorrowful

penning: writing the words to

phenomenal: extraordinary

picket: guard

pleurisy: an illness of the lungs causing pain in breathing

pored: read or studied attentively

poultices: heated, moist material

prematurely: before his due date

press-gang: men sent ashore by naval officers from Royal Navy warships to kidnap British citizens to serve on the ship

prestigious: well-known

privileged: enjoying benefits and advantages

proceeds: funds collected from the sale of the book

procured: obtained

proficiency: skills

prominent: famous

providence: divine intervention

providentially: happening from divine intervention

pseudonym: a fictitious name, especially one used by an author

pub: a public house that served drinks and food

reconnoitering: a preliminary survey to gain information

reproached: disgraced, shame

Root & Cady Music Company: a successful Chicago-based music publishing company

rugby: English football

scarlet fever: an infectious bacterial disease especially affecting children

severe erysipelas: an acute bacterial infection causing high fevers

singed: slightly burnt or scorched

sixpence: about six cents

spacious: roomy, large

stanzas: divisions of a poem

stem: restrain

subside: become gradually less intense

summoned: called

tenement house: a building with apartments on each floor, with a shared entrance stairway access

tuberculosis: disease caused by bacteria usually effecting the lungs

typhoid fever: an infectious bacterial disease contracted from contaminated food or water

valedictorian: the highest academic achiever of the class

variations: differences

Vicar: bishop

wadding: pieces of cloth or paper used between the powder and the bullet to prevent it from dropping into the powder charge, holding it in place in the barrel

Westminster Shorter Catechism: a concise summary of Christian doctrine formulated in the 17th century, primarily aimed at instructing children

William Cowper: an 18th century English poet and Anglican Hymnwriter

William Wilberforce: a British politician who led the fight to abolish slavery and the slave trade in British possessions

wretched: extremely bad or distressed

YMCA: Young Men's Christian Association

Corresponding Curriculum

Legends of Faith Series

Famous Hymnwriters • **Book 4**

All the stories in this book can correspond with the following Master Books Curriculum:

- A Child's Geography *(Series)*
- The World's Story *(Series)*
- Language Lessons for a Living Education *(Series)*
- Stobaugh's American and World History *(Series)*
- History of Religious Liberty
- The Annals of the World
- Adams Chart of History
- Foundations in Worship

Endnotes

1 Jane Stuart Smith and Betty Carlson, *Favorite Men Hymnwriters* (Wheaton, IL: Crossway Books, 1993), 111.

2 Douglas Bond, *The Poetic Wonder of Isaac Watts* (Sanford, FL: Reformation Trust, 2013), 6.

3 Smith and Carlson, *Favorite Men Hymnwriters*, 110.

4 Bond, *The Poetic Wonder of Isaac Watts*, 8.

5 Ibid., 15.

6 Ibid., 15.

7 Ibid., 29.

8 Ibid., 44.

9 Smith and Carlson, *Favorite Men Hymnwriters*, 168.

10 Bond, *The Poetic Wonder of Isaac Watts*, 46.

11 David Fountain, *Isaac Watts Remembered.* (Worthing: Henry E. Walter Ltd., 1974), 58.

12 Isaac Watts, *Watts's Divine and Moral Songs* (London, UK: D.D. Sampson Low, Son, and Marston, E. Matthews Publisher, 1836), 41–42.

13 Ibid., 8.

14 Bond, *The Poetic Wonder of Isaac Watts*, 68.

15 Ibid., 125.

16 Ibid., 129.

17 Ibid., 133.

18 Randy Peterson, *Be Still My Soul* (Carol Spring, IL: Tyndale House Publishers, 2014), 85

19 David Luckman, *John and Charles Wesley: Two Brothers, One Faith* (Scotland, UK: Christian Focus Publications, 2024), 28.

20 Ibid. 41.

21 Charles Wesley, *Charles Wesley's Journal, Volume 1* (Grand Rapids, MI: Baker Book House, 1980), 92.

22 Luckman, *John and Charles Wesley: Two Brothers, One Faith, 78*

23 Ibid., 78.

24 Ibid., 78.

25 Ibid., 78.

26 Jane Stuart Smith and Betty Carlson, *Favorite Men Hymnwriters* (Wheaton, IL: Crossway Books, 1993), 120.

27 T. Crichton Mitchell, *Charles Wesley: Man with the Dancing Heart* (Kansas City, MO: Beacon Hill Press, 1994), 93.

28 Luckman, *John and Charles Wesley: Two Brothers, One Faith*, 112.

29 Randy Peterson, *Be Still My Soul: The Inspiring Story behind 175 of the Most-Loved Hymns* (Carol Stream, IL: Tyndale House Publishers, 1973), 107.

30 Luckman, *John and Charles Wesley: Two Brothers, One Faith*, 141.

31 Anne Sandberg, *John Newton: Author of Amazing Grace* (Uhrichsville, OH: Barbour Publishing, 1945), 63.

32 Janet and Geoff Benge, *John Newton: Change of Heart* (Seattle, WA: YWAM Publishing, 2018), 81.

33 Noel Davidson, *How Sweet the Sound: The Absorbing Story of John Newton and William Cowper* (Belfast, Ireland: Ambassador Publishing Co, 1997), 10.

34 Randy Peterson, *Be Still My Soul* (Carol Stream, IL: Tyndale House Publishers, 2014), 27.

35 Davidson, *How Sweet the Sound: The Absorbing Story of John Newton and William Cowper*, 15.

36 Ibid., 18.

37 Sandberg, *John Newton: Author of Amazing Grace*, 158.

38 Davidson, *How Sweet the Sound: The Absorbing Story of John Newton and William Cowper*, 33.

39 Ibid., 37.

40 Benge, *John Newton: Change of Heart*, 148.

41 Ibid., 150.

42 Peterson, *Be Still My Soul*, 27.

43 Sandberg, *John Newton: Author of Amazing Grace*, 189.

44 Benge, *John Newton: Change of Heart*, 187.

45 Sandberg, *John Newton: Author of Amazing Grace*, 200.

46 Ibid., 201.

47 Benge, *John Newton: Change of Heart*, 199.

48 Rachel Phillips, *Well With My Soul* (Uhrichsville, OH: Barbour Publishing, 2003), 116.

49 John Piper, *The Hidden Smile of God* (Wheaton, IL: Crossway Books, 2001), 85.

50 Ibid., 118.

51 Charles J. Doe, *William Cowper's Olney Hymns* (Minneapolis, MN: Curiosmith, 2010), 11.

52 Phillips, *Well With My Soul*, 125.

53 Ibid., 126.

54 Noel Davidson, *How Sweet the Sound* (Belfast, Ireland: Ambassador Books, 1997), 48.

55 Piper, *The Hidden Smile of God*, 91.

56 Ibid., 59.

57 Ibid., 64.

58 Ibid., 72.

59 Ibid. 95.

60 Phillips, *Well With My Soul*, 136.

61 Ibid., 137.

62 Ibid., 137.

63 Davidson, *How Sweet the Sound*, 101.

64 Ibid., 141.

65 Phillips, *Well With My Soul*, 160.

66 Lucille Travis, *Fanny Crosby: The Blind Girl's Song* (Scotland, UK: Christian Focus Publications, 2013), 164.

67 Ibid., 9.

68 Bernard Ruffin, *The Hymnwriter Fanny Crosby* (Uhrichsville, OH: Barbour Books, 1945), 14.

69 Ibid., 16.

70 Fanny Crosby, *Fanny Crosby: An Autobiography* (Grand Rapids, MI: Baker Book House, 1986), 15.

71 Ibid., 32.

72 Travis, *Fanny Crosby: The Blind Girl's Song*, 18.

73 Ibid., 25.

74 Crosby, *Fanny Crosby: An Autobiography*, 37.

75 Ruffin, *The Hymnwriter Fanny Crosby*, 27.

76 Crosby, *Fanny Crosby: An Autobiography*, 44.

77 Ruffin, *The Hymnwriter Fanny Crosby*, 58.

78 Crosby, *Fanny Crosby: An Autobiography*, 130.

79 Ibid., 132.
80 Ruffin, *The Hymnwriter Fanny Crosby*, 85.
81 Crosby, *Fanny Crosby: An Autobiography*, 162.
82 Ibid., 162.
83 Ruffin, *The Hymnwriter Fanny Crosby*, 93.
84 Ibid., 93.
85 Ibid., 93.
86 Crosby, *Fanny Crosby: An Autobiography*, 188.
87 Ibid., 202.
88 Travis, *Fanny Crosby: The Blind Girl's Song*, 127.
89 Ruffin, *The Hymnwriter Fanny Crosby*, 109.
90 Travis, *Fanny Crosby: The Blind Girl's Song*, 140.
91 Travis, *Fanny Crosby: The Blind Girl's Song*, 140.
92 Ibid., 155.
93 Ruffin, *The Hymnwriter Fanny Crosby*, 95.
94 Travis, *Fanny Crosby: The Blind Girl's Song*, 155.
95 Ruffin, *The Hymnwriter Fanny Crosby*, 95.
96 Ibid., 196.
97 Travis, *Fanny Crosby: The Blind Girl's Song*, 163.
98 Ibid., 166.
99 Troi Penwell, *It Is Well* (Monee, IL: CreateSpace Independent Publishing Platform, 2018), 57.
100 Ibid., 64.
101 Rachel Phillips, *It Is Well with My Soul* (Uhrichsville, OH: Barbour Publishing, 2003), 11.
102 Ibid., 12.
103 Ibid., 13.
104 Ibid., 20.
105 Phillips, *It Is Well with My Soul*, 33.
106 Ibid., 34.
107 Randy Peterson, *Be Still My Soul* (Carol Stream, IL: Tyndale House Publishers, 2014), 153.
108 Ibid., 36.
109 Ibid., 36.
110 Ibid., 38.
111 Ibid., 51.
112 Phillips, *It Is Well with My Soul*, 61.
113 Randy Peterson, *Be Still My Soul* (Carol Stream, IL: Tyndale House Publishing, 2014), 195.
114 Ibid., 195.
115 Janet Grierson, *Frances Havergal: Worcestershire Hymnwriter* (Bromsgrove, Worcester, UK: The Havergal Society, 1979), 1.
116 Rachel Phillips, *Well With My Soul* (Uhrichsville, OH: Barbour Publishing, 2002), 169.
117 Ibid., 169.
118 Lucille Travis, *Frances Ridley Havergal: The Girl Who Loved Mountains* (Scotland, UK: Christian Focus Publications, 2014), 27.
119 Phillips, *Well With My Soul*, 172.
120 Ibid., 173.
121 Grierson, *Frances Havergal: Worcestershire Hymnwriter*, 41.

122 Travis, *Frances Ridley Havergal: The Girl Who Loved Mountains*, 54.

123 Ibid., 58.

124 Phillips, *Well With My Soul,* 184.

125 Ibid., 184–185.

126 Travis, *Frances Ridley Havergal: The Girl Who Loved Mountains*, 80.

127 Ibid., 84.

128 Ibid., 120.

129 Grierson, *Frances Havergal: Worcestershire Hymnwriter*, 148.

130 Ibid.,197.

131 Ibid., 202.

132 Travis, *Frances Ridley Havergal: The Girl Who Loved Mountains*, 155.

133 Travis, *Frances Ridley Havergal: The Girl Who Loved Mountains*, 156.

134 Ibid., 156.

135 Ibid., 156.

136 Grierson, *Frances Havergal: Worcestershire Hymnwriter*, 148.

137 Peterson, *Be Still My Soul*, 196.

138 Ed Reese, *The Life and Ministry of Philip Bliss* (Glenwood, IL: Fundamental Publishers, 1975), 5.

139 Ibid., 5.

140 Rachel Phillips, *It Is Well With My Soul* (Uhrichsville, OH: Barbour Publishing, 2003), 66f.

141 Ibid., 67.

142 Reese, *The Life and Ministry of Philip Bliss*, 6.

143 Phillips, *It Is Well With My Soul*, 68.

144 Ibid., 73.

145 J.H. Hall, *Biography of Gospel Song and Hymnwriters* (London, England: Forgotten Books, 2018), 179.

146 Phillips, *It Is Well With My Soul*, 80.

147 Reverend Elias Nason, *Lives of Moody, Sankey, and Bliss* (Philadelphia PA: B.B. Russell, 1877), 266.

148 Phillips, *It Is Well With My Soul*, 80.

149 Ibid., 81.

150 Ibid., 81.

151 Reese, *The Life and Ministry of Philip Bliss*, 13.

152 Phillips, *It Is Well With My Soul*, 81.

153 Ibid., 82.

154 Ibid., 89.

155 Reese, *The Life and Ministry of Philip Bliss*, 12.

156 Hall, *Biography of Gospel Song and Hymnwriters*, 181.

157 Nason, *Lives of Moody, Sankey, and Bliss*, 276.

158 Phillips, *It Is Well With My Soul*, 101.

159 D. W. Whittle, ed., *Memoirs of Philip P. Bliss* (Chicago, IL: A.S. Barnes & Company, 1877), 80.

160 Ibid., 166–167.

161 Ibid., 81.

162 Phillips, *It Is Well With My Soul*, 110.

163 Nason, *Lives of Moody, Sankey, and Bliss*, 286.

164 Ira Sankey, *My Life and the Story of the Gospel Hymns* (Philadelphia, PA: P. W. Zeigler & Company, 1906), 13.

165 Kelley Deegan Bruss, *Ira Sankey: Singing the Gospel* (Greenville, SC: Journey Forth Publishing, 1975), 12.

166 Sankey, *My Life and the Story of the Gospel Hymns*, 16.

167 Ibid., 16–17.

168 Ibid., 18.

169 Ibid., 21.

170 Bruss, *Ira Sankey: Singing the Gospel*, 35.

171 Sankey, *My Life and the Story of the Gospel Hymns*, 50.

172 Ibid., 54.

173 Bruss, *Ira Sankey: Singing the Gospel*, 106.

174 Ibid., 106.

175 Ibid., 107

176 Randy Peterson, *Be Still My Soul* (Carol Stream, IL: Tyndale House Publishers, 2014), 283.

177 Ibid., 283.

178 Bruss, Ira Sankey: *Singing the Gospel*, 141.

179 Ibid., 146.

180 Julia Ann Flora, *Suffering and Song* (North Canton, OH: Gracednotes Ministries, 2019), 18.

181 Randy Peterson, *Be Still My Soul* (Carol Stream, IL: Tyndale House Publishers, 2014), 15.

182 Ibid., 15.

183 Ibid., 61.

184 Jane Stuart Smith and Betty Carlson, *Great Christian Hymnwriters* (Wheaton, IL: Crossway Books, 1997), 162.

185 Peterson, *Be Still My Soul*, 210.

186 Kenneth W. Osbeck, *Amazing Grace* (Grand Rapids, MI: Kregel Publications, 1990), 187.

187 J.H. Hall, *Biography of Gospel Song and Hymnwriters* (London, UK: Forgotten Books, 2018), 72.

188 Ibid., 73–74.

189 Ibid., 75.

190 Smith and Carlson, *Great Christian Hymnwriters*, 86.

191 Osbeck, *Amazing Grace*, 248.

192 Peterson, *Be Still My Soul*, 207.

193 Osbeck, *Amazing Grace*, 348.

ISBN 13: 978-1-68344-400-8

ISBN 13: 978-1-68344-401-5

ISBN 13: 978-1-68344-402-2

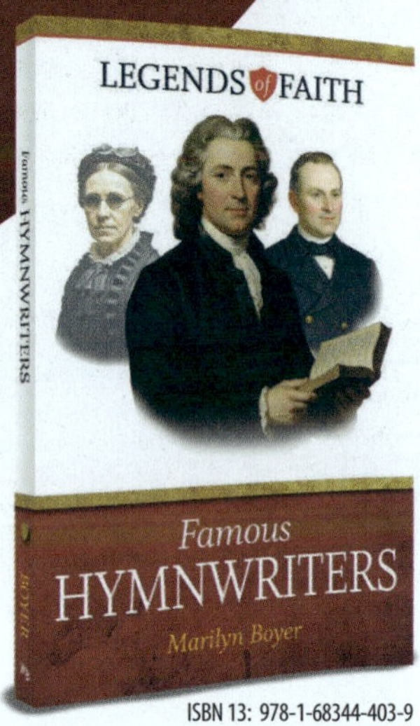

ISBN 13: 978-1-68344-403-9